H. A. REY

Find the Constellations

SECOND EDITION

HOUGHTON MIFFLIN HARCOURT
BOSTON • NEW YORK

**To Maria,
my favorite student
of the stars**

A note on Pluto: Because many objects have been discovered beyond Pluto in the last fifteen years, in 2006 an international group of astronomers voted to change the way we define planets and other objects in our solar system. Based on the new definitions Pluto has been reclassified as a dwarf planet and is no longer considered the ninth planet in our solar system.

A planet by definition is a celestial body that orbits the sun, is large enough for its own gravity to give it a nearly round shape, and is not a satellite of another planet. A planet has also cleared the neighborhood around its orbit, meaning that it has gravitationally attracted or repelled all other nearby objects of comparable size.

A dwarf planet by definition is a celestial body that orbits the sun, is large enough for its own gravity to give it a nearly round shape, is not a satellite of another planet, but does not clear the neighborhood around its orbit.

Second edition updates on the solar system and our planets, pages 56–59, provided by Ian Garrick-Bethell, Copyright © 2008, Houghton Mifflin Company

Copyright © 1954, 1962, 1966, 1976 by H. A. Rey
Copyright © renewed 1982 by Margret Rey
Planet-Finder update for the years 2007–2016
on page 65 provided by Chris Dolan

Library of Congress Cataloging-in-Publication Data is on file.

HC ISBN-13: 978-0-547-13140-5
PA ISBN-13: 978-0-547-13178-8

Printed in China
WKT 10 9 8 7 6 5 4 3 2 1

Few people can tell one star from another. Most of us can tell an oak from a maple or a jay from a woodpecker even though we don't see woodpeckers often, but the stars, which we see any clear night, remain a mystery to us.

Yet it is not difficult to know them. Simple shepherds 5,000 years ago were familiar with the heavens; they knew the stars and constellations — and they could not even read or write — so why don't you?

It is good to know the stars, if only to enjoy better the wonderful sight of the starry sky. But you simply must know them if you are interested in space travel.

This book helps you do it. It shows you how to recognize the stars and find the constellations that one can see in the middle and northern United States (about lat. 40°). It is a book to be used indoors and outdoors, all year round. It gives you views of the sky as if you were looking out at night through a huge observatory window. From these "sky views" you first pick out the stars and constellations one by one, and then you are ready to go out and find them in the real sky. Before long you will feel as much at home among the stars as you do in your own backyard.

And now, happy stargazing!

3

CONTENTS

dog

hare

Well what do you know—
a DOG in the sky!

At night time, when the stars are out, the sky all of a sudden becomes a huge picture book. You can look up and see a lion and a whale, an eagle, a swan, a dog, a hare, and a lot of other pictures; that is, of course, if you know how to find them.

Those pictures are made by the stars, and finding them is a wonderful game. Let us start the game with a picture you may have heard of, or maybe you have seen it yourself: the Big Dipper.

In the sky, the Big Dipper looks like this — just a group of seven bright stars. Now, how do we make it a dipper? Well, all we do is draw some lines between the stars like this

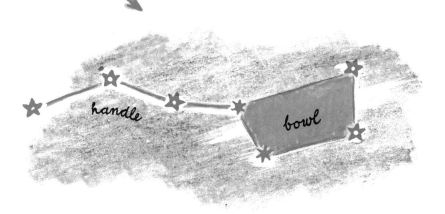

and there it is, a dipper with a handle and a bowl. The stars in both pictures are exactly the same — you check them! — but the lines in the lower one help us find the shape. Look at the upper drawing again; can you see the dipper, even without those lines?

Sure I can see it!

THE GREAT BEAR

The next picture we are going to find is the Great Bear. Around the Big Dipper there is a group of stars like this:

This does not look like much but watch what happens if we draw our lines; not just any lines, of course, but the right kind. It becomes a bear!

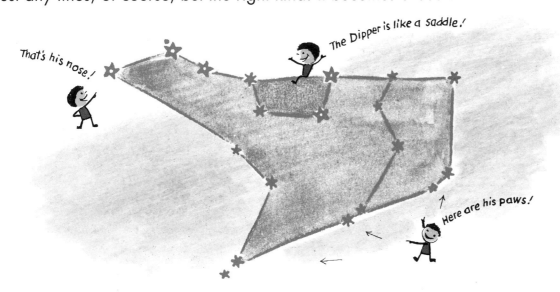

Here is the Great Bear. The Great Bear is a constellation. Constellations are groups of stars that form shapes in the sky; they were given their names many hundreds of years ago. The Big Dipper is a part of the constellation Great Bear.

THE HERDSMAN

Not far from the Great Bear is another constellation, the Herdsman, and this is what it looks like:

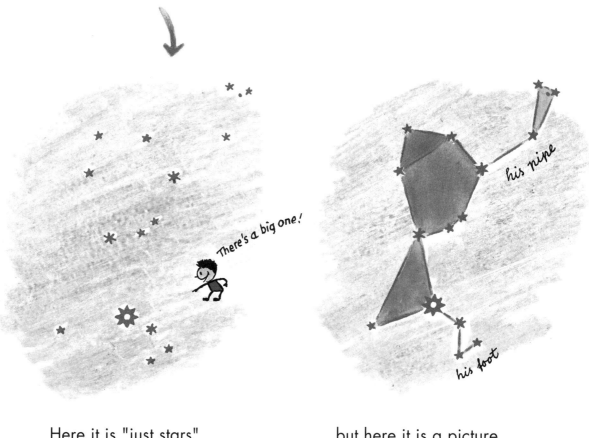

Here it is "just stars" but here it is a picture

It's a man with a large head who is sitting down and smoking a pipe. Can you make out the Herdsman in the drawing to the left by filling in the lines in your imagination? If you can't, why not take a piece of tracing paper and fill them in with a pencil.

THE LION

Here is another constellation. It is called the Lion and it looks like this before we draw our lines:

and now it's a rather good matchstick lion:

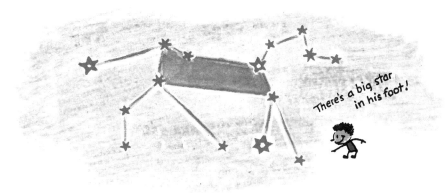

There's a big star in his foot!

Can you see his tail and body and head and four legs? Can you "see" the figure in the upper drawing when you put your hand over the drawing below? You can if you try.

By the way, do you notice that the stars on these pages are not all alike? Some are big, some small, some in between. On the next page we shall see why.

BRIGHT STARS AND FAINT STARS

We can't make the stars in our book look all alike because the *real* stars in the sky don't look alike. Some are bright, some just fairly bright, some are very faint. Just watch the sky tonight and see for yourself how different they are.

Now, when you want to find a constellation in the sky you always pick the bright stars first and then you go on to the fainter ones. That is the easiest way. From the constellations in the book you can tell which stars are bright, which faint, and which in between.

The stars have "grades" according to their brightness. Those grades are called "magnitudes." The brightest stars are called "1st magnitude stars." The fairly bright ones are of 2nd magnitude, then 3rd, then 4th, and the very faint ones are of 5th magnitude (as you see, these grades run the opposite way from grades at school). Here's a list to show how the different magnitudes are marked on our constellation figures:

Great Bear has no 1st-mag. star!

Herdsman and Lion have 1st-mag. stars!

STARS HAVE NAMES

The brightest stars all have names, like tall buildings or mountaintops. The very bright star in the Herdsman is called Arcturus, and the bright one in the Lion, Regulus (stress on *Reg*).

It's a good idea to remember the names of the brightest stars and it is easy, since there are not many. There are only 15 stars of 1st magnitude in our northern skies. We shall meet them all.

All star names are Latin or Greek or Arabic and that's why some of them sound funny. One star, for instance is called Betelgeuse. You pronounce it like "beetle juice" but it has nothing to do with juice for beetles. It's Arabic and means "giant's shoulder." We shall meet that star in a moment.

And now let's do a few more constellations.

Don't constellations have Latin names too?

Sure! You find them in the Index.

THE TWINS

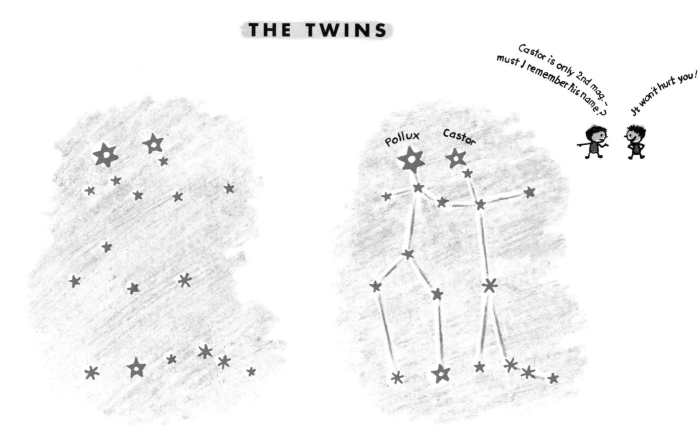

Here are the stars of the Twins, and here is the figure: two matchstick men holding hands, each with a bright star in his head; Castor to the right and Pollux to the left. Can you tell the magnitudes of the stars in this group?

The Twins are in the zodiac (stress on *zo*) and so is the Lion, whom we met on page 9. The zodiac is that part of the sky where we can see the planets. Therefore the zodiac is important for anybody who is interested in space travel. We shall hear more about the zodiac and the planets later on.

ORION

This constellation is named for Orion (stress on *ri*), who was an ancient Greek hunter and warrior. The figure does look like a warrior, with a club and a shield, and a sword dangling from the belt. Orion's belt, with its three bright stars in a row, is a landmark of the winter sky. Maybe you knew it already.

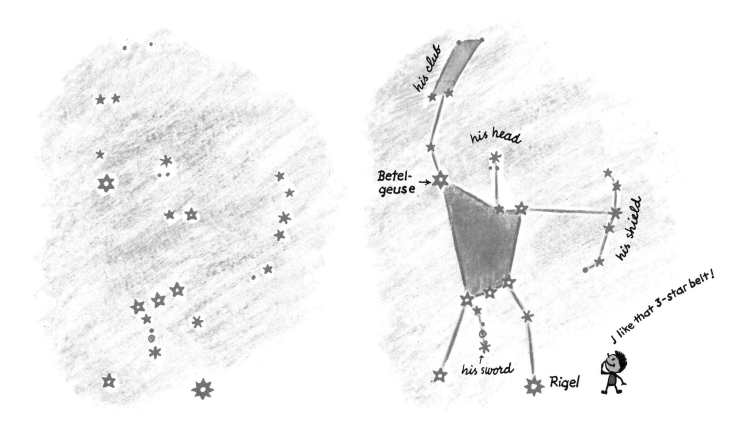

Orion has more bright stars than any other constellation. Two are 1st-magnitude stars: Betelgeuse (remember?) and Rigel. Rigel is a giant star, more than 40 times as large across as our sun and 16,000 times as bright. Yet in the sky it looks only like a pinpoint of light because it is so tremendously far away: 545 light-years. On the next page we shall see what a light-year is.

LIGHT-YEARS

To begin with, a light-year is not a "year" but a "distance." It is the distance light travels in a year.

Light is the fastest thing there is. It travels 186,000 miles a second, and in a year almost six million million miles. In numbers this would read 6,000,000,000,000 miles. So many zeros would get anyone mixed up. It is easier to say or write "1 light-year" than to use all those millions of millions of miles.

Now if we say the star Rigel is 545 light-years away, it means that its light took 545 years to get here. It left Rigel before Columbus discovered America and traveled all those years through space to reach us. And it would take us 545 years to get from Earth to the star Rigel if we had spaceships which had the speed of light.

Of course we have no such ships. A space rocket about to leave Earth only does about 5 miles a second. Against the speed of light that's just snail's pace.

Space rocket: about 5 miles a second   Light: 186,000 miles a second

Because all stars are millions of millions of miles away we always measure their distance in light-years.

None of the other stars we have met up to now are as far away as Rigel. Arcturus is only 32 light-years away, Regulus 70, Pollux 31, Castor 44, and Betelgeuse 300.

Only one star is so near that we don't have to use light-years. It is "only" 93 million miles away, and its light reaches us in about 8 minutes. You know that star. It is our sun.

The sun is a star too, like the ones you see shining in the sky at night: all stars we see, including the sun, are tremendous balls of fiery gas, each of them hundreds of thousands or even millions of miles across. The reason they don't look as big and bright to us as our sun is just that they are so very far away. A house or a tree or a mountain looks smaller from far away than nearby, and it is the same with a star.

It is hard to visualize such distances but this is how you can get at least a rough idea: if we imagined the distance was only one inch from Earth to sun instead of 93 million miles, then a light-year on the same scale would be one mile, and the nearest star in our skies, Sirius (which we'll meet on the next page), would be 8½ miles away on this scale.

A light-year
is 63,290 times as long
as the distance
from Earth to sun.

EARTH   SUN

See what I mean?

A mile
is 63,360 times as long
as an inch.

0   ½   1 inch

But let's get back to our constellations.

From now on we won't have to draw each constellation twice — with lines and without. You surely get the idea by now.

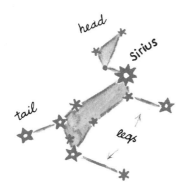

This is the Big Dog. He has a remarkable dog tag: the 1st-mag. star Sirius, by far the brightest of all stars. You cannot miss Sirius, it is so brilliant. Sirius is only 8½ light-years away, nearer than any other star we can see from most parts of the United States.

There is also a Little Dog. He has only two stars and does not make much of a figure. At best it could be a pup's tail But one of the stars, Procyon (stress on *Pro*), is of 1st mag. and very bright, so well remember it. Procyon is "only" 10 light-years away. That's nearby, as stars go.

This is the Charioteer, the chariot driver. He looks tough but that is natural because chariots are battle wagons. His eye is a very bright star, Capella, of 1st mag., which is 42 light-years away.

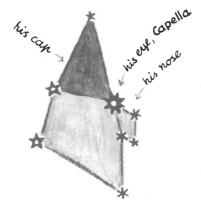

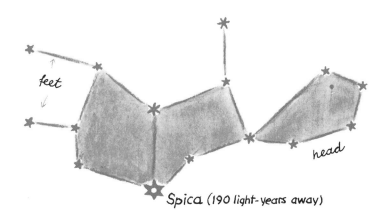

Spica (190 light-years away)

The Virgin looks like a woman lying down, with a large head and a short skirt. Only one of her stars is bright: Spica, of 1st mag. As you can see on page 39, her head is right below the Lion's tail. Maybe she is scared and that's why she is raising her arm.

claws

Antares

sting

tail

The Scorpion has two claws and a curved tail ending in a sting, like a real scorpion. His main star, 1st-mag. Antares (stress on *tar*) is also a giant star, even bigger than Rigel, more than 200 times as large across as the sun, and 170 light-years away. It has a striking reddish color. Perhaps you have never noticed that the stars do have different colors. Sirius is bluish, Capella yellowish, and Betelgeuse reddish, but none is as colorful as Antares. The two stars close together in the Scorpion's sting are called the "Cat's Eyes." There is an ancient story about the scorpion and the hunter Orion, which you will find on page 42.

Scorpion and Virgin are both in zodiac, that part of the sky where the planets can be seen.

Attention, space men!

Here is a **QUIZ:** Can you name these constellations?

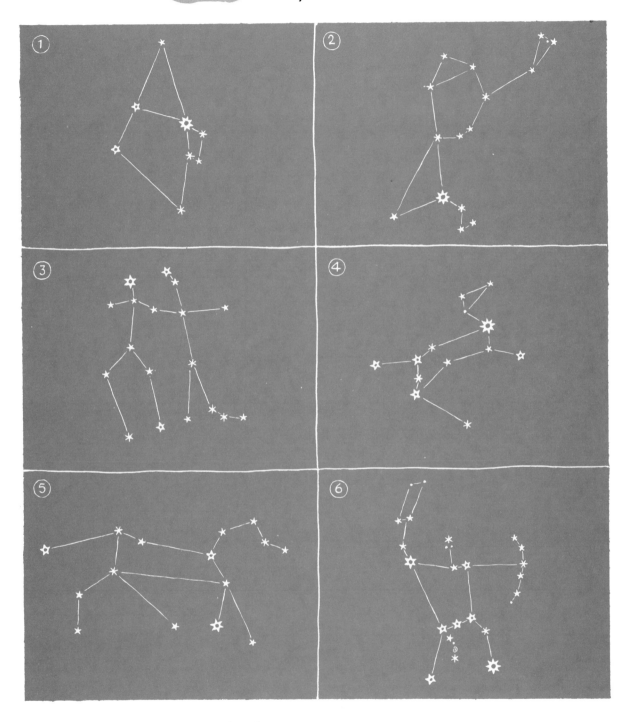

1: Charioteer 2: Herdsman 3: Twins 4: Big Dog 5: Lion 6: Orion

Here are the same constellations ~~without lines~~ — but not in the same order.
Can you tell which constellation is which, and the full names of the stars?

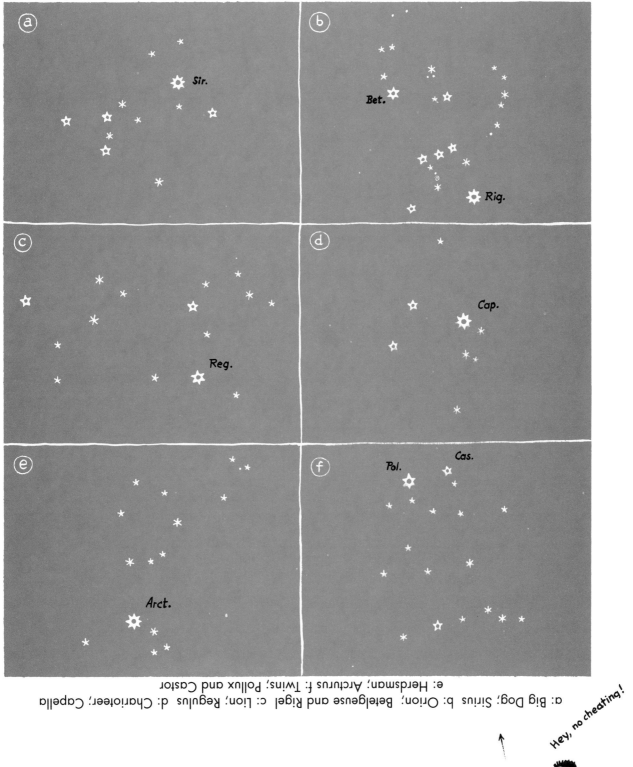

Hey, no cheating!

If you are a Boy Scout or Girl Scout and want to earn a merit badge in astronomy you must know ten constellations, four of them in the zodiac. That's exactly what we know by now. But we shall do even better. Right now we'll meet five more constellations with 1st-magnitude stars, and then we shall have met all those that have 1st-magnitude stars in them. Here are three of them:

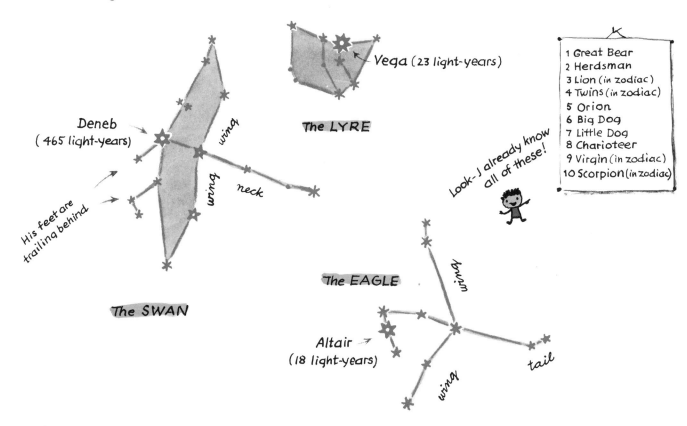

Deneb
(465 light-years)

wing

wing

neck

His feet are
trailing behind

The SWAN

Vega (23 light-years)

The LYRE

Look- I already know
all of these!

1 Great Bear
2 Herdsman
3 Lion (in zodiac)
4 Twins (in zodiac)
5 Orion
6 Big Dog
7 Little Dog
8 Charioteer
9 Virgin (in zodiac)
10 Scorpion (in zodiac)

The EAGLE

wing

Altair
(18 light-years)

wing

tail

The Swan and the Eagle are flying toward each other with their wings spread out. The Swan is stretching his neck forward the way real swans do in flight. In the Swan's tail is the star Deneb, of 1st-magnitude. Deneb is Arabic and means just that: tail.

The Eagle's head has three stars in a row, with 1st-mag. Altair (stress on *tair*) in the middle. The three stars in a row are easy to recognize.

The Lyre looks like a small harp with two strings. The ancient Greeks played the lyre the way we play the guitar, to accompany songs. In the Lyre is the 1st-mag. star Vega, bluish white, the third-brightest in the northern skies. Vega is famous: it was the first star to have its photograph taken, in 1850.

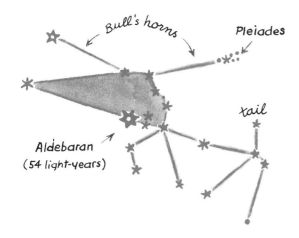

Bull's horns

Pleiades

tail

Aldebaran
(54 light-years)

This is the Bull. Besides the 1st-mag. star Aldebaran (stress on *deb*) it has another special attraction, the Pleiades (stress on *Ple*), a small group of stars so close together that at first glance they look like a tiny silver cloud. The Pleiades are a lovely sight. Don't miss them. The Bull is in the zodiac.

The last of our 15 brightest stars is Fomalhaut (stress on *Fom*) in the Southern Fish. The rest of this small constellation is so dim that we won't bother with it.

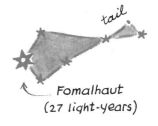

tail

Fomalhaut
(27 light-years)

Thus we have met the 15 brightest stars of our skies. Here they are again, in order of their brightness: Sirius, the most brilliant of all; Arcturus; Vega; Capella; Rigel, the faraway giant star; Procyon; Betelgeuse, with the odd name; Altair; Aldebaran; Antares, the red giant; Spica; Pollux; Fomalhaut; Deneb; and Regulus. Do you recall the constellations they are in?

And now, before we go on, how about another Quiz?

Smile, please!

Vega

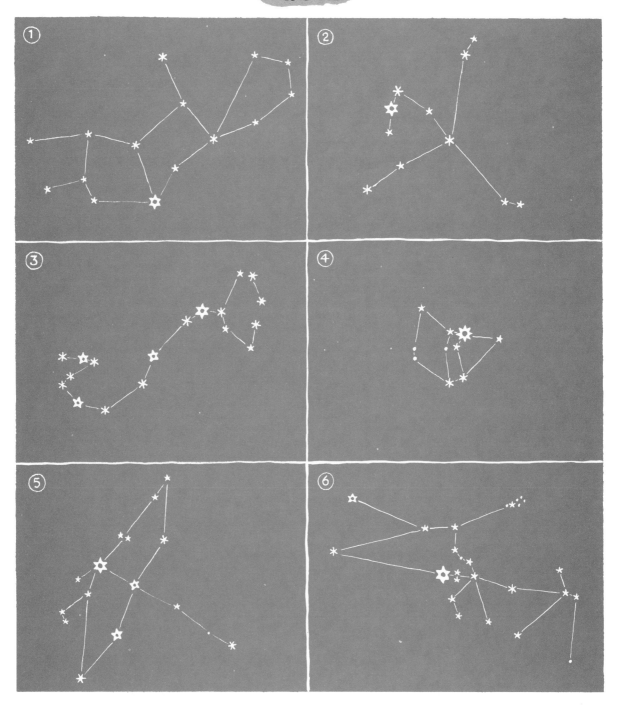

Can you name the constellations, and the bright star in each one?

1: Virgin; Spica 2: Eagle; Altair 3: Scorpion; Antares
4: Lyre; Vega 5: Swan; Deneb 6: Bull; Aldebaran

QUIZ

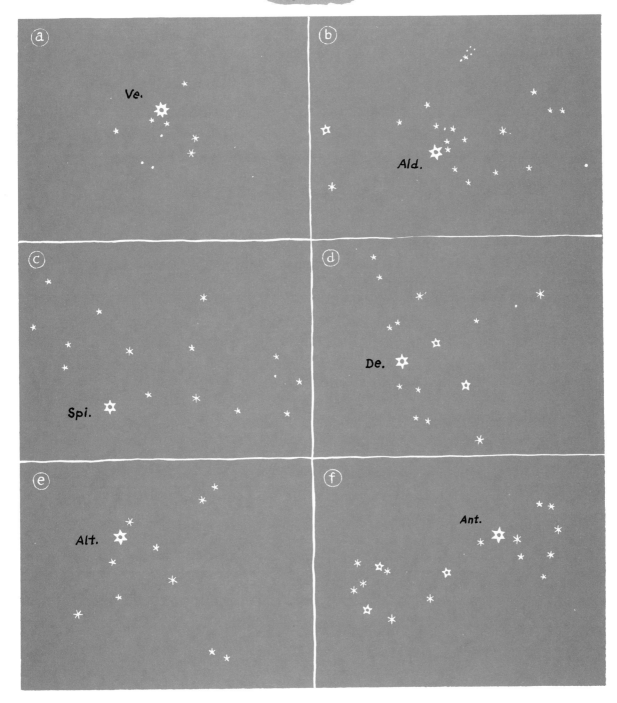

Here are the same figures, in different order. Also, some of them are twisted. Can you tell which constellation is which, and the full names of the stars?

a: Lyre; Vega   b: Bull; Aldebaran   c: Virgin; Spica
d: Swan; Deneb   e: Eagle; Altair   f: Scorpion; Antares

That's easy!

23

Where must I look for the Lion?

THE SKY VIEWS

If we want to find the constellations in the sky it is not enough to know their shapes. We must also know where to find them.

The stars that make up the constellations are spread out over the whole sky. What we need, therefore, are pictures of the whole sky where we can see the constellations in relation to each other. For this we have the sky views.

We have different sky views for different times of the year. If you live in the city and don't often see the stars, you perhaps did not know that the starry sky looks different at different times of the year or even at different hours of the same night — but it does. That's why we need different sky views.

We have four sets of sky views in this book, one for each season, beginning in winter because our year starts in winter. Each set has two sky views: one shows that half of the sky which you see as you are facing north; the other shows the half you see as you are facing south.

Each sky view is a double page. The left-hand page shows the stars only, without lines, the way you would see them in the real sky. The right-hand page shows exactly the same stars but with lines connecting them so you can recognize the constellations.

What we want to do is to find the constellations on the "stars only" pages. In the beginning you will have to look at the "with lines" page for every figure you want to spot, but soon you won't have to do that so often, and in the end you will find that you can recognize the constellations on the "stars only" pages at a glance. Then you are ready to find the constellations outdoors in the real sky.

And now stop reading for a moment and look at the sky views on the next four pages. You don't have to read the text below the views — you can do that later. Just see whether you can find some of the 15 constellations we have already met. It won't take long, perhaps five minutes. Then come back here and read on.

Ready? How did you make out? How many constellations did you find?

Did you notice that there were a lot of constellations we have not met yet? There are more than 50 constellations in our skies; so far we don't even know a third of them! We shall meet a few more but by no means all. Quite a few are faint or small, and we don't have to bother with them. They are on our sky views because the sky views are like road maps. A good road map shows not only great cities and highways but also smaller roads and villages, so our sky maps must show also the lesser figures, not only the bright and important ones.

And now let's skip the next four pages with Sky View I, since we have just looked at them, and go right on to meet a few more of the important stars and constellations.

THE SKY LOOKS LIKE THIS AROUND

If this time does not suit you,

December 15 ...
January 1 ....
January 15 .....
February 15 ....
March 1 ....

**Here are the stars
the way you see them in the sky —**

Can you find the Big Dipper on this page? It's easy. First you spot it on the opposite page and then you look for it in exactly the same place on this page. Then look for Polaris, then for the bright star high up, and so on. Take your time. There's no hurry.

Perhaps you think there are more stars on this page than on the opposite one, but it only seems so. The number of stars is exactly the same on both pages; you check them!

MAGNITUDES:

1   2 3 4 5

STARS

FEBRUARY 1, ABOUT 9 P.M.

you can see the same sky on:

... about midnight
... about 11 p.m.
... about 10 p.m.
... about 8 p.m.
... about 7 p.m.

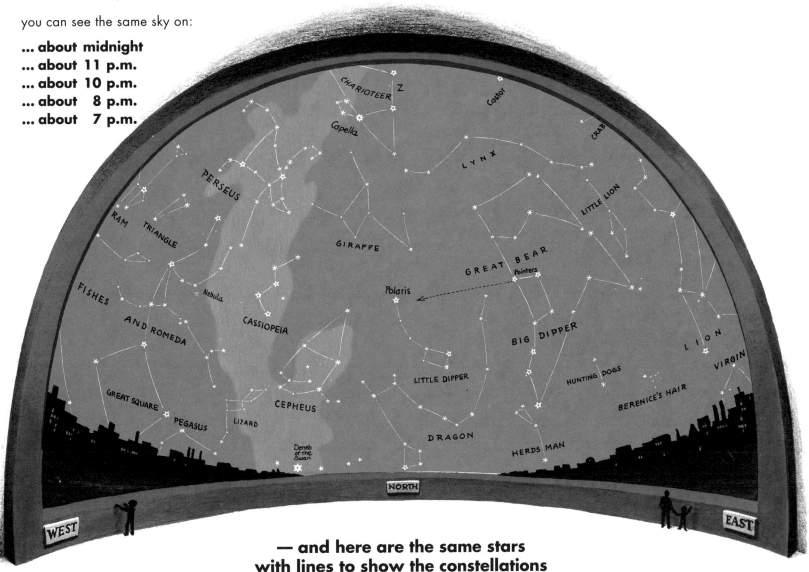

**— and here are the same stars
with lines to show the constellations**

There are not so very many stars on our sky views anyway. There are fewer than 400 on Sky View I, north and south together. The sky is not as full of stars as most people think. Ask your friends how many they guess they can see: they will guess too high. Even on the clearest night one can't see more than, say, 2,500 stars at a time with the naked eye, and most of them are so faint they aren't even on our sky views. With telescopes it's different, of course; with them one can see millions.

W I N T E R

THE SKY LOOKS LIKE THIS AROUND

If this time does not suit you,

December 15 ...
January 1 ....
January 15 .....
February 15 ....
March 1 ....

**Here are the stars
the way you see them in the sky —**

Merry Xmas!

On this sky view you are looking at the most splendid region of the whole sky. One could call it "Christmas sky" because it looks like this around midnight on Christmas. There are 8 stars of 1st magnitude: can you spot them? If you are far south in the U.S., in Los Angeles, say, or New Orleans, you may see another very bright star low above the horizon, below Sirius. That's Canopus (stress on *no*), second brightest star in the entire sky. Canopus is not on the sky views because they are designed for a latitude of 40° north. Too bad one cannot make

MAGNITUDES:

1　2 3 4 5

STARS

FEBRUARY 1, ABOUT 9 P.M.

you can see the same sky on:

... about midnight
... about 11 p.m.
... about 10 p.m.
... about 8 p.m.
... about 7 p.m.

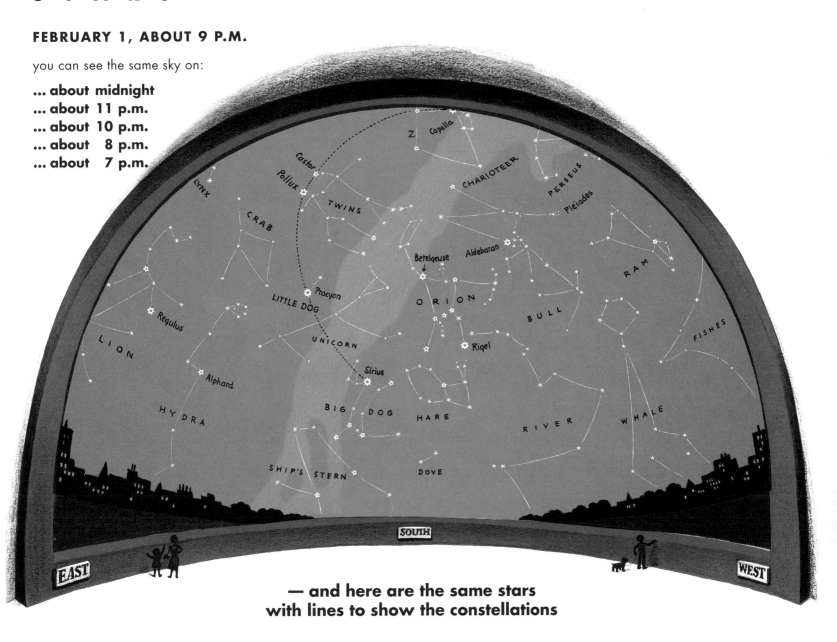

**— and here are the same stars
with lines to show the constellations**

a good sky chart that fits all latitudes. Sirius, Procyon, Pollux, Castor, and Capella form the "Great Arc of Sirius." Try to trace it. It's easy.

The irregular band of lighter blue on this and other sky views is the Milky Way, a beautiful sight on clear, dark nights. Before telescopes were invented, about 350 years ago, nobody knew for sure what it was, but with modern telescopes we see that it is made up of billions of stars, too far away to be seen singly with the naked eye. We shall hear more about it on page 53.

POLARIS, THE NORTH STAR

There is one star that is very important even though it is not one of the 15 brightest, being only of 2nd magnitude. It is a famous star. You probably know its name already or you have even seen it: the star is Polaris, the Pole Star.

Now what makes Polaris so important? It is this: Polaris (stress on *lar*) is the only star that never changes its place in the sky, at least not so that you can notice it. It always stays put while the other stars and constellations are moving.

Polaris is also called the North Star. Why? Because it is always north. When you are looking at Polaris you are facing north, and to your right is east, to your left west, and south is behind you. This is important to know not only for stargazing but for another reason: suppose you lose your way at night. If you can find the North Star you know your directions right away. You won't need a compass.

Polaris is easy to find in the sky. All you do is look for the Big Dipper and draw a line from the two stars in the bowl the way the drawing on page 30 shows, and you will hit Polaris. There's no bright star near Polaris so you can't miss it. The two stars in the bowl which point to the Pole Star are called the Pointers. No matter how the Dipper stands, high or low, the Pointers always point toward Polaris. (On the sky views it's even easier to find Polaris: it is always on the same spot in the middle of the sky views facing north.)

I won't get lost — I can find the North Star!

And how about all other stars, which appear to move while Polaris stands still? (We say "appear to move" for they don't really move. It's because the earth spins around its axis that they seem to move; you probably learned this at school.) Well, they seem to go around Polaris in circles. It takes them 24 hours, almost, to go around Polaris once. Those near Polaris run smaller circles, those far from it, larger ones. Stars far from Polaris show up above the horizon for a while only. The farther from Polaris they are the shorter is the time they are above the horizon. Some don't show up above the horizon at all in this country, except in the southernmost parts — the famous Southern Cross, for instance. One must travel far south to see them, so they are not on our sky views.

When a star comes up above the horizon we say it rises. When it goes down we say it sets. Like the sun and the moon the stars rise in the east and set in the west. Most stars and constellations rise and set. Only a few run their circles around Polaris entirely above the horizon. They may be high or low in the sky but they never rise or set, and we can see them at all times. The Big Dipper is one of them, and we shall meet the others on the next page.

Here are the constellations around the Pole Star — except the Big Dipper, which we know already:

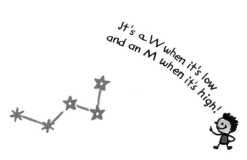

This is the Little Dipper, with Polaris at the tip of the handle. It is also called Little Bear but it looks more like a dipper.

This is Cassiopeia (stress on *pe*). It sometimes looks like a W and sometimes like an M. It is fairly bright and easy to find in the sky. Cassiopeia was an ancient queen. Below we'll meet her husband.

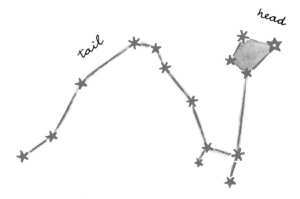

The Dragon has a long tail and a four-star head. His snout is a 2nd-mag. star but his other stars are dim.

Cepheus (stress on *Ceph*) was an ancient king and Cassiopeia's husband. He is wearing a pointed hat and has a pigtail. He is not bright but looks rather gay, perhaps because there is a happy ending to the romance of his daughter Andromeda, which we shall hear on page 40.

The Giraffe is a very faint figure. We won't have to bother with it except to say hello.

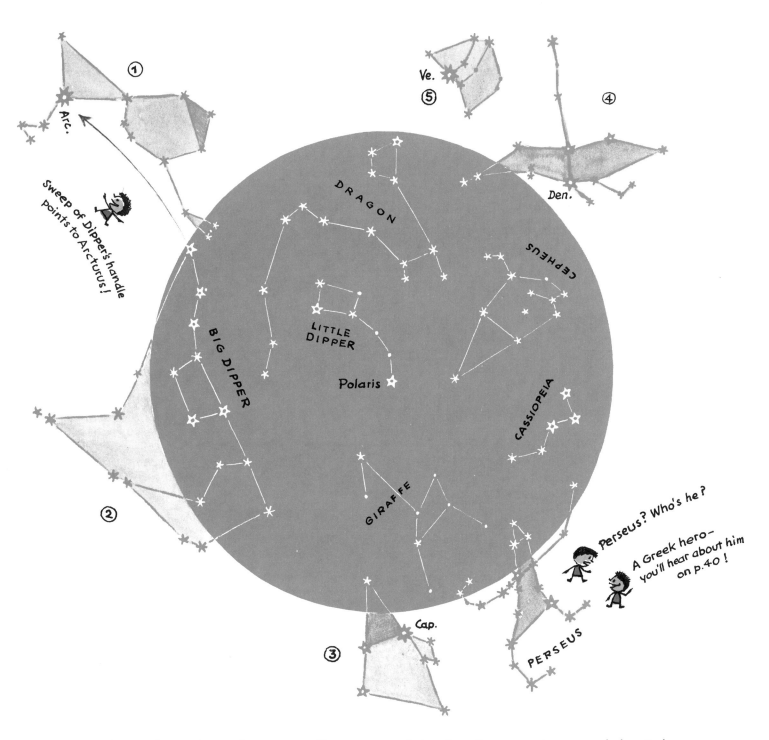

This is how those five constellations, and the Big Dipper, sit around the Pole Star. The stars within the blue circle are always above the horizon in our latitudes (about 40° north). A few of our old acquaintances are close to the circle and partly within it. Can you name them?

1: Herdsman 2: Great Bear 3: Charioteer 4: Swan 5: Lyre

THE ZODIAC CONSTELLATIONS

The zodiac, as we have heard before, is that part of the sky where we can see the planets. It is a sort of belt going all around the sky, made up of twelve constellations. These are the names of the twelve zodiac constellations:

Ram, Bull, Twins,
Crab, Lion, Virgin,
Scales, Scorpion, Archer,
Goat, Water Carrier, Fishes

Want to memorize them? Look for jingle on p. 71!

Five of the zodiac constellations we have met before. (Do you remember which? They all had 1st-magnitude stars.) Here are the other seven, which are new to us:

The Archer is the only one of them which is quite bright even though it has no 1st-magnitude stars. It's a man in a long skirt, with a feather on his head, leaning forward and aiming a bow. He is aiming at the Scorpion (see sky view page 47), and we shall later find out why.

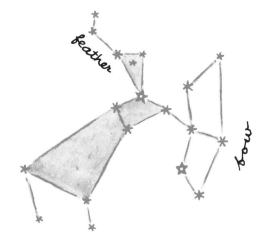

The other six figures consist mainly of faint stars. We should not bother about them if they were not in "Planet Lane"— the zodiac. Here they are:

Zodiac got anything to do with Zoo?

Sure! Both come from the same Greek word, and Zodiac means Animal Circle.

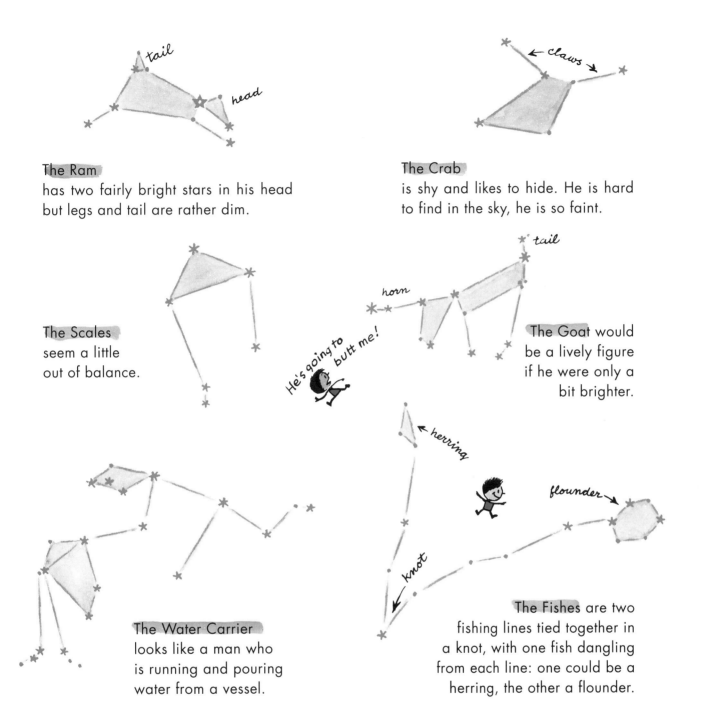

The Ram
has two fairly bright stars in his head
but legs and tail are rather dim.

The Crab
is shy and likes to hide. He is hard
to find in the sky, he is so faint.

The Scales
seem a little
out of balance.

The Goat would
be a lively figure
if he were only a
bit brighter.

He's going to butt me!

The Water Carrier
looks like a man who
is running and pouring
water from a vessel.

The Fishes are two
fishing lines tied together in
a knot, with one fish dangling
from each line: one could be a
herring, the other a flounder.

And now, how about another look at the sky views to see whether we can find
the constellations we have met on the last four pages.

S P R I N G

THE SKY LOOKS LIKE THIS AROUND

If this time does not suit you,

March 15 ....
April 1 ....
April 15 ......
May 15 ....

z

WEST   NORTH   EAST

Here are the stars
the way you see them in the sky —

Just for sport, can you find the Big Dipper on this sky view without looking at the opposite page? Don't try too hard, though. It's easier if you look at page 37 first and then come back here and find the two Dippers, and Polaris. Look for the 1st.-mag. stars in this sky view; there are five. What are their names? Compare the figures on page 37 with those on page 27: do you see how the Big Dipper is now much higher up and Cassiopeia much lower down than they were on Sky View 1? Perseus has almost set, but the Swan, which was all

No Milky Way on this
Sky View! Why?

MAGNITUDES:

1 2 3 4 5

S T A R S

MAY 1, ABOUT 9 P.M.

you can see the same sky on:

... about midnight
... about 11 p.m.
... about 10 p.m.
... about 8 p.m.

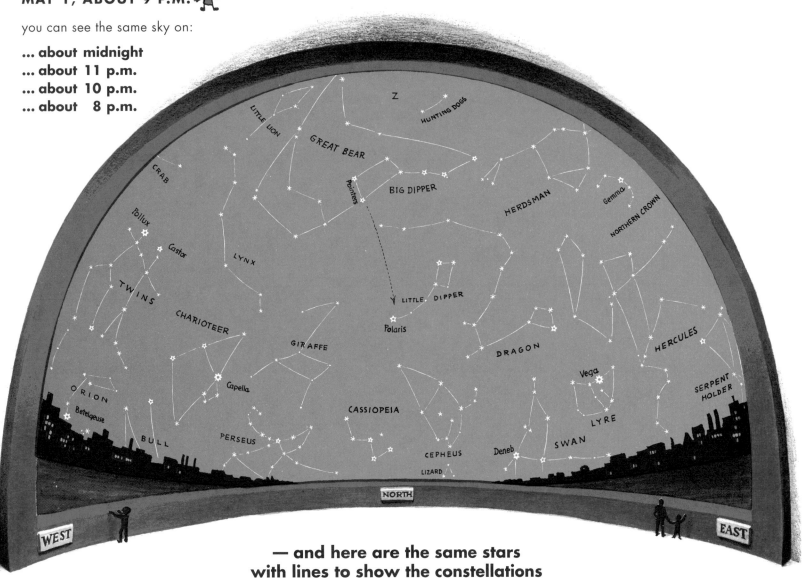

**— and here are the same stars
with lines to show the constellations**

but gone on page 27, is rising. Being not far from Polaris, he does not remain long below the horizon. The Herdsman is high up now (see also page 39). On page 27 only his pipe was showing.

At this time of year many parts of the country are on Daylight Saving Time. If you are, remember to add 1 hour to the figure on the time table above (which is your Standard Time). So, read 10 p.m. instead of 9 p.m., 1 a.m. instead of midnight, etc., if you go stargazing outdoors.

SPRING

THE SKY LOOKS LIKE THIS AROUND

If this time does not suit you,

March 15 ....
April 1 ....
April 15 ......
May 15 ....

Here are the stars
the way you see them in the sky —

Here again you see the change if you compare with Sky View 1, south. The stars you saw there have either moved westward, like the Lion, or set altogether, like the Big Dog. But new figures have risen in the east, Virgin and Scales; and the Scorpion's claws are showing above the horizon. There are some constellations here we have not met. None of them have very bright stars, but let's just say hello to two of them. Below the Virgin is Hydra, the Water Snake, very long and faint. Her brightest star, Alphard, is only of 2nd mag. but seems brighter

MAGNITUDES:
☼ ☆ ☆ ★ ⁎ ⁎
1   2 3 4 5

STARS

For D.S.T. add 1 hour!

MAY 1, ABOUT 9 P.M.

you can see the same sky on:

... about midnight
... about 11 p.m.
... about 10 p.m.
... about 8 p.m.

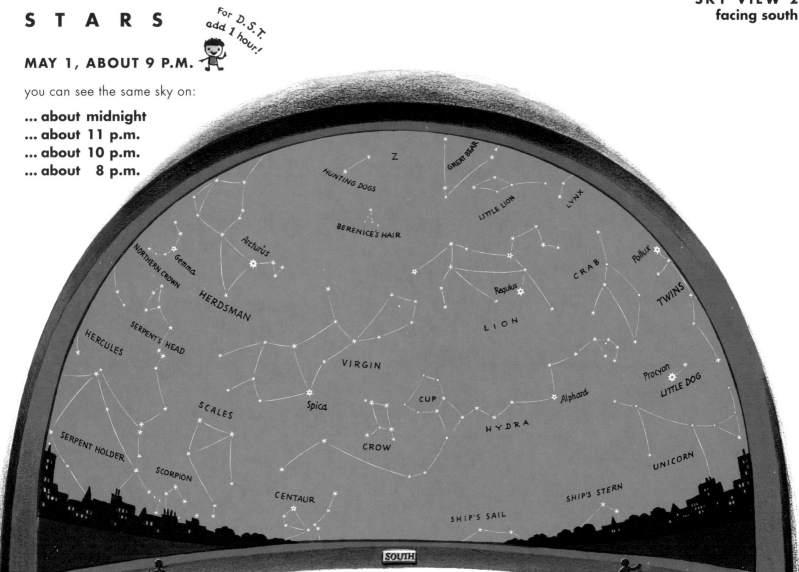

— and here are the same stars
with lines to show the constellations

because the stars around it are dim. Near the back of the Herdsman's head is the Northern Crown, small but pretty, and easy to find in the sky. It looks more like a tiara, though, than a crown.

In late spring, orange-colored Arcturus is the first star you see come out, high up in the sky, before it has become quite dark. It is fun to watch the first stars come out, any time of the year, and it's even more fun if you know them by name and know where in the sky to look for them. If you have company play it as a game: who can identify the first star?

Nice game – but what stars will first be out in other months?

Look at the list on page 66!

THE ANDROMEDA STORY

There are many ancient myths about the stars and constellations. One of them has to do with King Cepheus and Queen Cassiopeia (we met them on page 32), and with their daughter Andromeda (stress on *drom*). Do you want to hear it? Then listen.

Young Andromeda was a beautiful girl, so beautiful that Queen Cassiopeia boasted her daughter was more beautiful than the Sea Nymphs. Now the Sea Nymphs were goddesses and disliked being compared with a mere mortal princess, so they complained to Neptune, the highest Sea God. Neptune promptly sent out a monstrous whale, who swam along the shores of the King's realm devouring his subjects by the dozen. Nobody was able to fight the monster, and there seemed no way to get rid of him except — so the King was told — by sacrificing Andromeda, the lovely princess.

So Andromeda was chained to a rock by the sea and left to her fate. Presently the whale emerged from the waves to swallow her. But just at this moment a hero, Perseus, passed by. He killed the whale, freed Andromeda, and married her on the spot. Then the two went off on Perseus' winged horse, Pegasus (stress on *Peg*).

This story was first told thousands of years ago, but to this day you can see them in the sky as constellations: the King, the Queen, the Princess, Perseus, Pegasus, and the Whale. They are all in the same region of the sky, and when Cassiopeia is high up, on autumn evenings, all the other figures of this story can be seen too. (See Sky View 4, pages 50–53.)

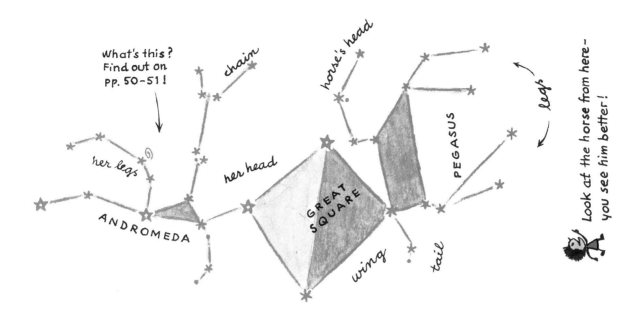

What's this? Find out on pp. 50–51!

chain

horse's head

her legs

her head

ANDROMEDA

GREAT SQUARE

PEGASUS

leg

wing

tail

Look at the horse from here – you see him better!

Here are Andromeda and Pegasus. The princess is wiggling her legs and holding up one arm, with a chain on it. The horse has a large wing attached to his rump. The three stars of the wing and the one in the princess's head are fairly bright. They make a square, the famous Great Square of Pegasus. It is a landmark of the autumn sky and not hard to find. Try it when the time is right, some autumn evening.

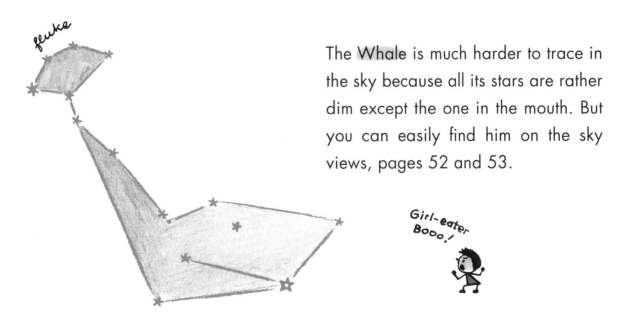

fluke

The Whale is much harder to trace in the sky because all its stars are rather dim except the one in the mouth. But you can easily find him on the sky views, pages 52 and 53.

Girl-eater Booo!

THE ORION STORY

To tell all the stories about the constellations would fill a whole book, but we have room for one more, the one about Orion.

Orion, you recall, was a great hunter who roamed the earth with his two companions, the Big Dog and the Little Dog, which we met on page 16. Unfortunately, Orion was also a great braggart. He used to boast that no game could ever escape him. This annoyed the goddess Juno, so one day while Orion was pursuing a hare she had a scorpion sting his heel and Orion died.

Now there was a physician, Aesculapius (stress on *la*), the most famous doctor of all times. Supposedly he got some of his medical secrets from the snakes, and he usually carried one around. Aesculapius was called and lo! he brought Orion back to life.

But this was not the end. The god Pluto, King of the Dead, heard the news and got worried. What would become of his kingdom if the dead could be awakened by doctors? So he told his brother, Jupiter, about the case, and Jupiter promptly threw his thunderbolt and killed Orion, this time for good, and Aesculapius, too.

After that, everybody concerned was put into the sky among the stars: Orion with his two dogs, Aesculapius and his pet serpent, the Scorpion, and also the hare Orion had been hunting when he had the accident. As a precaution the Archer (see page 34) was posted near the Scorpion, and Orion and the

Scorpion were placed in opposite parts of the sky so they could never again get into trouble. Orion shines in winter, the Scorpion in summer, and when one rises the other sets, to this very day.

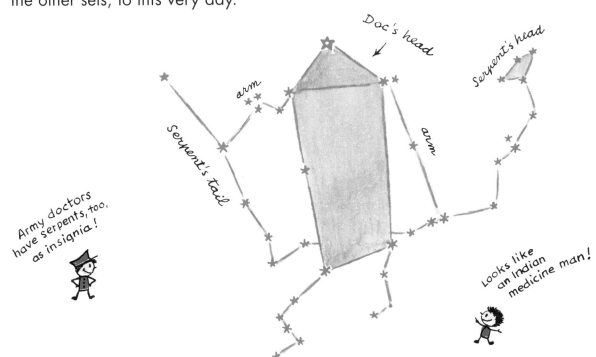

The Serpent Holder: the figure of the Doctor in the sky is called Serpent Holder because of the serpent in his hands. You find him easily on the sky views but you have to be good at stargazing to trace him in the real sky, for most of his stars are dim and far apart.

The Hare, on the other hand, has a few bright stars rather close together in his head and is not hard to spot in a clear winter night, below Orion's feet (see page 29).

On Sky View 3, pages 46–47, you find the Scorpion, with the Doctor and his serpent atop, and the Archer standing on guard to the left, ready to shoot his bow.

SUMMER

THE SKY LOOKS LIKE THIS AROUND

If this time does not suit you,

June 15 ....
July 1 ....
July 15 ....
August 15 ....
September 1 ....

**Here are the stars
the way you see them in the sky —**

Can you find the Big Dipper without looking at the next page? It is now to the left, or west, of Polaris, and Cassiopeia is to the right, or east; the opposite of what it was on Sky View 1, page 27; have a look and compare the two! And look also for a moment at page 51, with the Big Dipper low down and Cassiopeia high up. When you compare all four northern sky views (pages 27, 37, 45, 51) you can see how the constellations near Polaris wander around it, Polaris staying where it was, while those farther away dip below the horizon in

MAGNITUDES:

1   2 3 4 5

S T A R S

For D.S.T.
add 1 hour!

AUGUST 1, ABOUT 9 P.M.

you can see the same sky on:

... about midnight
... about 11 p.m.
... about 10 p.m.
... about 8 p.m.
... about 7 p.m.

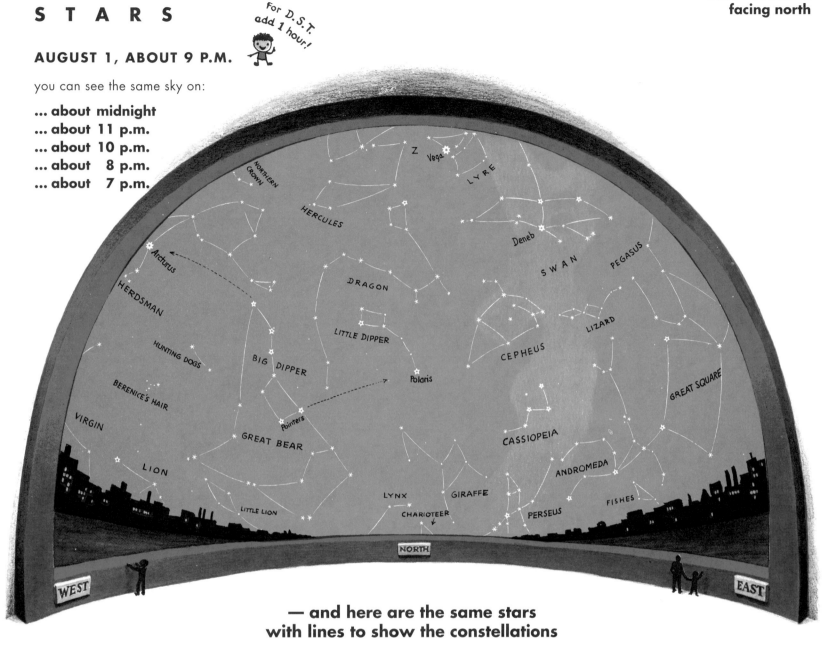

— and here are the same stars with lines to show the constellations

the west and then come up again in the east.

This is a good time to find the Dragon. His head is high up, near the zenith, the point directly overhead, marked on all sky views by a tiny "Z."

If you are outdoors look at the middle star in the Big Dipper's handle. There is a faint star very close by, riding on it. The two are called "Horse and Rider." You can see the Rider almost any time of the year, and the ancients used it as an eye test: if you could see it your vision was all right.

S U M M E R

THE SKY LOOKS LIKE THIS AROUND

If this time does not suit you,

June 15 ....
July 1 ....
July 15 ....
August 15 ....
September 1 ....

z

SOUTH

EAST   WEST

**Here are the stars
the way you see them in the sky —**

High up in the Milky Way, Swan and Eagle are flying toward each other, and above the southern horizon the Archer is aiming his bow at the Scorpion, with its beautiful red star Antares. Look for Antares when you are outdoors on the Fourth of July. Then it is almost exactly south at 9 p.m. Standard Time (10 p.m. Daylight Saving Time). Try also to spot the "Cat's Eyes" in the Scorpion's tail. With lots of patience you may be able to trace the Serpent Holder. If you can do it, you are really good! Vega, Altair, and Deneb form the famous "Summer Triangle,"

MAGNITUDES:

1 2 3 4 5

bang!

Stop those firecrackers! I want to see Antares, the 4th of July-star!

S T A R S

AUGUST 1, ABOUT 9 P.M.

For D.S.T. add 1 hour!

you can see the same sky on:

... about **midnight**
... about **11 p.m.**
... about **10 p.m.**
... about **8 p.m.**
... about **7 p.m.**

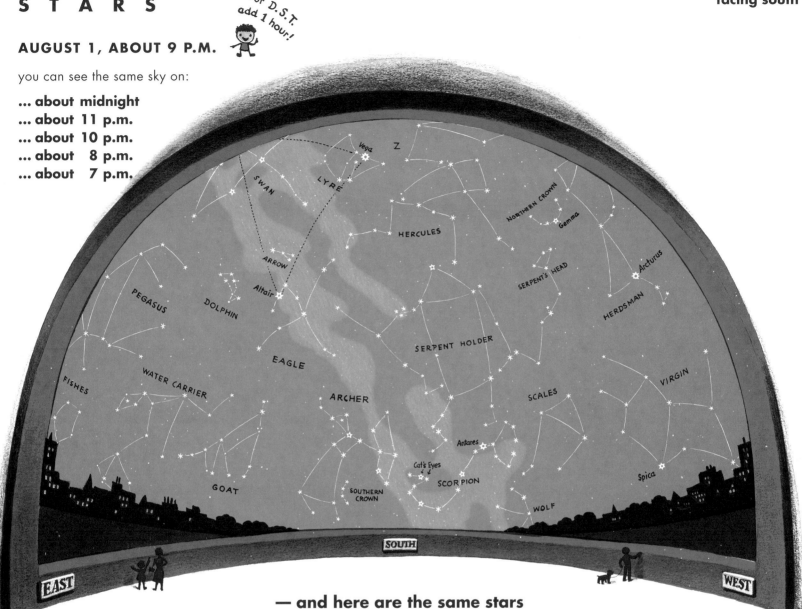

**— and here are the same stars
with lines to show the constellations**

with a right angle at Vega. All navigators know it. It is easy to find.

Above the Serpent Holder is one of the constellations we have not met before: Hercules (stress on *Her*), the man with the club. Hercules was a Greek hero famous for his strength, but as a constellation he is rather weak, without bright stars. Don't bother about him much but try to find the Dolphin, a lovely little figure near the Milky Way, not far from the Eagle's head with its three stars in a row. The Dolphin is not hard to find, and you'll like him.

FOUR MINUTES A DAY

Nobody can tell the weather far in advance. Even the best weatherman can't tell if it's going to rain or shine a week from next Tuesday.

With the stars it is different. We can always tell in advance exactly what stars are going to be in the sky, not only weeks from now, but at any time: any hour of any night of any month of any year. We can do this because the stars have a schedule that is more reliable than any train schedule in the world, and as regular as clockwork. If we know about this schedule it helps us understand why we can see some stars or constellations at some times of the year and why we can't at other times.

Fortunately, the star schedule is very simple. So simple that it can be put in one sentence: A star — any star — rises and sets about four minutes earlier every day than it did the day before. That's all.

It sounds easy, you say, but why bother about those 4 minutes? What difference does it make? Well, those 4 minutes make a lot of difference because they add up. In a week, it's 7 times 4 minutes — 28 minutes. That is almost half an hour, and in a month it makes 30 times 4 minutes. That's 120 minutes, or two full hours.

So we can also put the schedule this way: every day the stars rise and set two hours earlier than they did a month ago. This means that after two months they rise four hours earlier; after six months, twelve hours earlier; and after twelve months, 24 hours earlier. Any child can figure that out. Twelve months is a year, and 24 hours is one full day, so after one year the same stars rise again at the same time as they did a year ago, and we are back where we started.

Let us take an example, the star Sirius for instance, and follow it through a year. On January 1, Sirius rises about 7:00 in the evening and sets about 3:00 in the morning. You can see it all the time if you stay up. Here is its schedule as it rises and sets two hours earlier from month to month:

JAN.   1:   rises at 7 p.m. and sets at 3 a.m.   *You can see Sirius almost all night!*
FEB.   1:   rises at 5 p.m. and sets at 1 a.m.
MAR. 1:   rises at 3 p.m. and sets at 11 p.m.   *Now you get just a glimpse of it in the evening!*
APR.   1:   rises at 1 p.m. and sets at 9 p.m.
MAY   1:   rises at 11 a.m. and sets at 7 p.m.   *Now it's up during daytime only— you can't see it at all!*
JUNE 1:   rises at 9 a.m. and sets at 5 p.m.
JULY 1:   rises at 7 a.m. and sets at 3 p.m.
AUG. 1:   rises at 5 a.m. and sets at 1 p.m.
SEPT. 1:   rises at 3 a.m. and sets at 11 a.m.   *Now you'll see it again if you stay up late—*
OCT.   1:   rises at 1 a.m. and sets at 9 a.m.
NOV. 1:   rises at 11 p.m. and sets at 7 a.m.   *— and now you can see it again almost all night!*
DEC.   1:   rises at 9 p.m. and sets at 5 a.m.
JAN.   1:   rises at 7 p.m. and sets at 3 a.m.

Thus a year is over and we are back where we started.

What goes for Sirius goes for the other stars too, and not only for their rising and setting. We can put it this way: wherever you see a star or a constellation in the sky — high up, low down, anywhere — you will see it in exactly the same place two hours earlier a month later, provided, of course, that it won't be daytime then so that you can't see the stars.

You can check this schedule on the time tables on each sky view. Sky View 1, for instance, is for 9 p.m. on February 1, and the stars you see there are the same ones you see at 11 p.m. on January 1, or at 7 p.m. on March 1.

49

AUTUMN

THE SKY LOOKS LIKE THIS AROUND

If this time does not suit you,

September 15..
October 1 ....
October 15 ......
November 15 ..
December 1 ....
December 15 ..

**Here are the stars
the way you see them in the sky —**

You have seen all the constellations on this sky view before. They have moved on of course, and will keep moving until, eventually, they will be back again in the position where we saw them on Sky View 1. And so they will run their course, season after season, year in, year out.

Do you see the little curlicue near Andromeda's knee, not far from the "Z" which marks the zenith? This is the famous Nebula (stress on *Neb*) of Andromeda.

MAGNITUDES:

1 2 3 4 5

S T A R S

NOVEMBER 1, ABOUT 9 P.M.

you can see the same sky on:

... about midnight
... about 11 p.m.
... about 10 p.m.
... about 8 p.m.
... about 7 p.m.
... about 6 p.m.

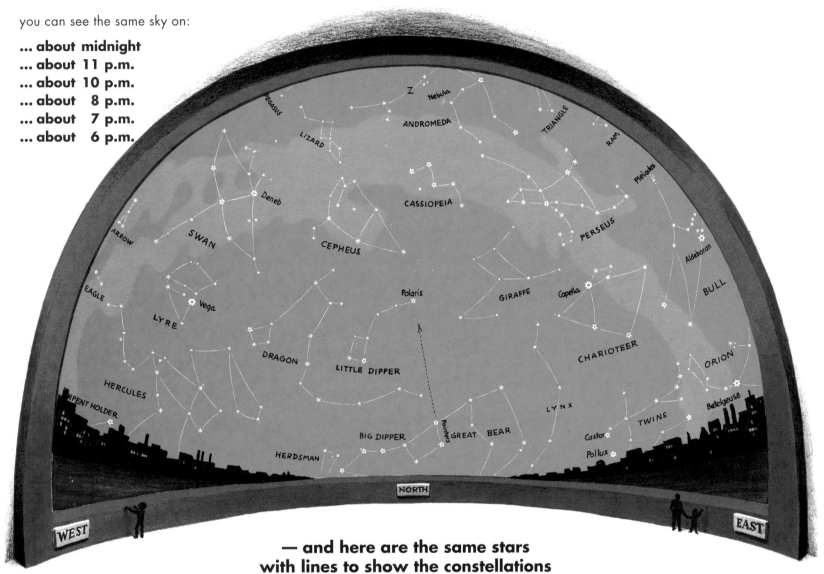

**— and here are the same stars
with lines to show the constellations**

You see it on clear, dark nights, a wisp of faint, hazy light. It is tiny yet it's worth looking for: it is the most distant object—the farthest-away thing—anybody can see with the naked eye. And this wisp of haze looking so small is in reality the biggest single object you can see. It is a galaxy (stress on *gal*), a gigantic swarm of stars, a hundred billion of them, far, far out in space, How far? Hold your breath: about 2.7 million light-years! The light from that galaxy,

Wow! How many miles is that?

About sixteen million million million miles!

THE SKY LOOKS LIKE THIS AROUND

If this time does not suit you,

September 15 ..
October 1 ....
October 15 ......
November 15 ..
December 1 ....
December 15 ..

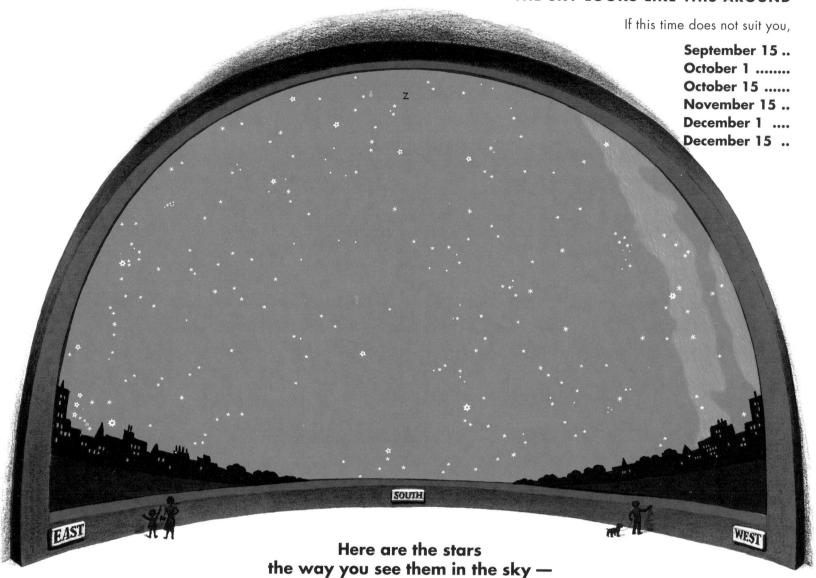

Here are the stars
the way you see them in the sky —

now reaching our eyes, left those distant stars about 2.7 million years ago, a million years before Stone Age men lighted the first fires and chipped the first stone tools.

There are countless such star swarms, or galaxies, in the vastness of space, but you would need a telescope to see them, for they all are millions of light-years away from us. In fact, the Andromeda Nebula, far away though it is, is one of the nearest galaxies, a neighbor of ours. We ourselves, our sun and its planets,

Hey, neighbor!

Nebula

MAGNITUDES:

1 2 3 4 5

STARS

NOVEMBER 1, ABOUT 9 P.M.

you can see the same sky on:

... about midnight
... about 11 p.m.
... about 10 p.m.
... about 8 p.m.
... about 7 p.m.
... about 6 p.m.

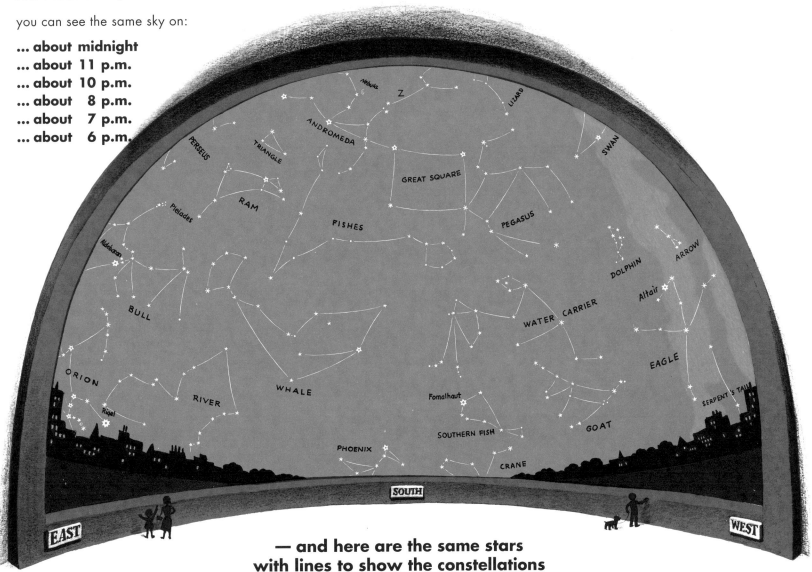

**— and here are the same stars
with lines to show the constellations**

and all the stars we see in the sky are within such a gigantic star swarm, our own galaxy.

This galaxy of ours is also made up of a hundred billion stars or more, and is shaped more or less like an enormous pinwheel, 100,000 light-years across, with streams of stars spiraling out from it. The rim of this "pinwheel" is what you see in the sky as the Milky Way.

STARGAZING OUTDOORS

Now that we are familiar with the shapes of the main constellations and with the brightest stars, let's go out and find them in the real sky. It's going to be fun. To get the most out of it, keep a few things in mind:

Polish remover
the paint off ac

❶ Take this book along and a flashlight to see the pictures in the dark. Paint the glass of the flashlight red with nail polish so the light won't blind you.

❷ Pick a place where trees, buildings, or street lights are not in your way. In the city, the roof of an apartment building makes a good observatory. But it must be safe, with walls or a fence around it.

❸ Pick the right hour with the help of the time table on page 67. It tells you which sky view to use, and at what hour to use it, on any date. This is important, otherwise you may have a hard time trying to find the constellations. After you have done some stargazing and know how the constellations look in the real sky you won't have to stick to these hours so closely.

❹ Pick a clear night, without a moon. A bright moon blots out all stars except the brightest ones, and you won't recognize many constellations. On exceptionally clear moonless nights you can see lots of very faint stars that are not on the sky views, since you don't need them to find the constellations. On the other hand, don't expect to find in the sky all the stars that are on your sky view. Some may be covered by a passing cloud, and near the horizon there is always a haze hiding the fainter ones.

❺ When you go out, look for the Big Dipper and the North Star first, to get your bearings. Face either north or south: that's the way the sky views are designed. And remember, always pick out the brightest stars first and check from the sky views which is which. At the beginning don't try to find too many constellations in one night. Four or five new ones each night are plenty.

Few stars tonight—
the moon is too bright!

6 When you watch the stars overhead, do sit or lie down, lest you get a crick in the neck. Lie down, too, if you want to look out for shooting stars (August is the best month for watching them), and bring a blanket, because the grass is often wet with dew on summer nights.

7 Finally, watch out for *planets*. Any bright star you see in the sky which is not on any of the sky views is probably a planet. Very likely it is one of these four: Venus, Mars, Jupiter, or Saturn. It could also be Mercury, but he is rarely visible, so we will leave him out.

You can tell the planets by their look. Venus is so much brighter than any true star that you recognize her at once. You can see her in the evening as a brilliant evening star, or before sunrise as a morning star, but never in the middle of the night, and she never is very high in the sky. Jupiter is not quite as bright but usually brighter than the rest of the stars, so he too is easy to spot. You can always tell Mars by his reddish color but his brightness varies much, from fairly bright to brilliant, depending on how near he is to Earth. Saturn is always quite bright and has a yellowish tinge. Jupiter and Venus are whitish.

As a rule you can see at least one planet any night, and often two or more at the same time. You always find them in or near one of the constellations of the zodiac. The Planet Finder on page 65 tells you at a glance where you may expect to see any of these four planets up to December 2016.

On the next pages let's find out a few more things about the planets.

THE PLANETS

You have often heard about planets in space stories, and you probably know that there are eight of them: Mercury, Venus, Mars, Jupiter, Saturn, Uranus (stress on *U*), Neptune, and our own Earth.

The first five of them we have just met. They are the ones you can see in the sky without a telescope. The chances are that you have often seen one or the other but did not realize you were looking at a plane! You probably thought it was just another star. For planets do look like stars, as we have seen. Yet they are not true stars. What then is the difference between stars and planets? Let's find out.

1. Stars are enormously far away, light-years or even hundreds or thousands of light-years. 2. Stars glow with their own light because they are enormously hot. 3. Most stars are enormously big; many stars are far bigger than our sun. 4. Stars do not change their places in the sky in relation to each other, for thousands of years; that's why they are called "fixed stars." The constellations are made up of fixed stars only, and move across the sky in a body, like planes in formation.

Planets are different: 1. Compared to the fixed stars they are close by. Not light-years but light-minutes or -seconds. Even Pluto, a distant dwarf planet, is thousands of times nearer than the nearest star. 2. The planets are not aglow with heat. They shine with borrowed light, the light of the sun, which they reflect. 3. The planets are small compared with any star you see in the sky, like peas or marbles compared with beach balls. 4. The planets wander. Over weeks and months or even years you see them slowly wander from one constellation of the zodiac to the next. They have no fixed place in the sky in relation to the stars, and that's why we cannot put them in our sky views.

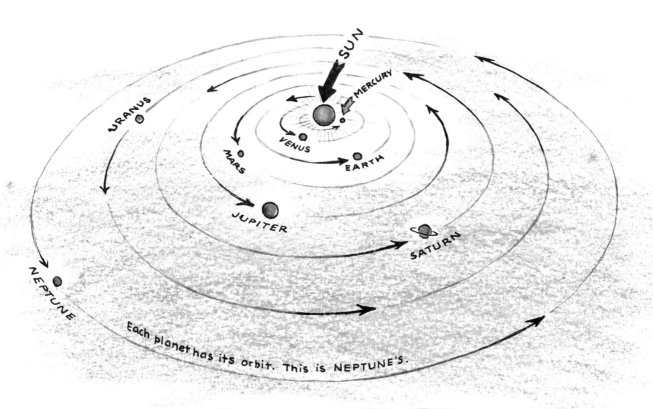

THE SOLAR SYSTEM

The planets, including Earth, circle around the sun. The sun and the planets circling around it make up our solar system. The planets go around the sun, each in its own path. The path of a planet is called the orbit; it never varies. The planets move around the sun at different speeds, and the time a planet takes to go once around is called a "year." Not only Earth but also Mercury, Venus, Mars, and the others have a year. The farther from the sun a planet is, the longer its year.

Some of the planets have satellites, or moons, which move around the planets just as the planets move around the sun. Earth's satellite is our moon. There are now many artificial satellites circling Earth, but they won't stay in orbit forever.

And now for a closer look at the planets on the next page.

Drawing above not true to scale—do not use for space navigation!

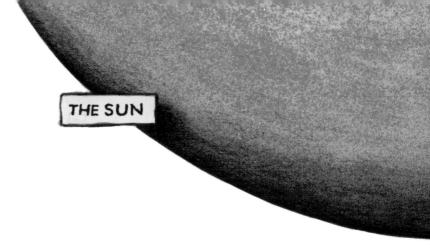

THE SUN AND THE PLANETS

Here are the sun and the eight planets, all drawn on the same scale. The planets are shown in the order of their distance from the sun. As you see, they differ very much in size but all are small compared to the sun.

The Sun: An enormous ball of fiery gases, 1,730,000 miles across, and tremendously hot: 10,000 degrees on the surface, and millions of degrees at the core. We can show only part of the sun here because even on the scale of this drawing, it would be too large (12 inches across) to fit the page.

Mercury: Baby among planets, only 3,032 miles across. Nearest to the sun, distance 36 million miles. Mercury's sunny side is so hot that lead would melt; his shady side may be 200° below zero. No place to spend a vacation. Goes around the sun in 88 days (1 Mercury year). Has no atmosphere, no satellite.

Venus: Almost as big as Earth, 7,521 miles across, second nearest to the sun, distance 67 million miles. Has very dense atmosphere, and it's very hot there, probably about 850° F, much hotter than boiling water (212°). Several probes have landed on Venus and found that it is a harsh, desolate world with no life. Can't see stars or the sun from Venus, for her thick clouds never lift. A Venus year is 225 days—Earth days, that is. Has no satellites.

← ⸻ [240,000 miles] ⸻ → ● Moon

Earth: Third nearest to the sun, 93 million miles away; 7,926 miles across. Goes around the sun in 365¼ days—our year, Earth's year. Fairly good place to live; if you know a better one, name it. Has one satellite, our moon, which is 2,160 miles across and about 240,000 miles from Earth. (Drawing shows moon's distance from Earth true to scale.)

How far from Earth to the sun on this scale? About 35 yards!

SCALE

0   50,000   100,000 miles

One million Earths wouldn't quite fill the Sun!

Mars: Fourth from the sun, 142 million miles. Much smaller than Earth; only 4,222 miles across. Very thin atmosphere and very cold, usually around 80° below zero, but sometimes as warm as 20° F. Pictures from rovers and orbiting space-craft show the surface is cratered like the moon, but also has valleys and polar ice caps like on Earth. No signs of life, so don't expect to see any Martians flying about in saucers when you land there. Martian year almost twice as long as Earth year: 687 days. Has two tiny moons, not more than 20 miles across.

Jupiter: Fifth, 484 million miles from the sun; giant among planets—almost 89,000 miles across. Very cold, 160° below zero. No place for a visit; perhaps you could land on one of its 63 moons, two of them bigger than Mercury, and one of which probably has a water ocean beneath a thick icy surface. Has a thin ring. Year is almost 12 Earth years long.

Saturn: Sixth, 887 million miles from the sun; also a giant—75,000 miles across. Besides at least 60 moons, has famous rings consisting of millions of tiny moonlets. Even colder than Jupiter, perhaps 220° below zero. Year is almost 30 Earth years long.

Uranus: Seventh, 1,784 million miles from the sun; 31,800 miles across. Temperatures 320° below zero; it's getting worse the farther away we get from the sun. Has at least 27 moons and goes around the sun in 84 years (1 Uranus year). It is surrounded by 13 thin, dark rings made of rock and ice.

Neptune: Eighth, 2,793 million miles from the sun; 30,800 miles across; has at least 13 moons and has thin rings. Neptune's year = 165 Earth years. Temperature more than 300° below. Brrr!

How about the asteroids? They're too small for this drawing- look them up on p.68!

Suppose you are in charge of a rocket ship and want to go to Mars. Once you have left Earth, in which direction would you go?

You answer: "That's simple! I head my ship toward Mars and keep it headed that way till I get there." Well, that's wrong, and this is why:

A trip to Mars will take many months (Mars is never less than 35 million miles from Earth), and while you are moving toward Mars, Mars is moving too, and fast! He moves along his orbit at more than 50,000 miles per hour. So don't try to chase him. You'll waste fuel and food and air and probably never catch up with him.

So what do you do? You must intercept Mars! You don't head for the point where you see Mars when you are leaving Earth. Instead, you take off in such a way that your ship will travel in an orbit of its own. This orbit is so calculated that it will touch the orbit of Mars in a certain point, and you must time your takeoff so that your ship will arrive at that point precisely at the moment when Mars will be there too.

Scientists will calculate your orbit, and also the exact time your trip will take; probably less than eight months. Most of the time you'll be coasting, but you will have to check your flight constantly and correct it with short rocket bursts. And how do you make those checks? The answer is <u>by the stars</u>. The stars are your road signs. You can always see them. Out in space they are never hidden by clouds.

Luckily the stars and constellations you see anywhere in the solar system are exactly the same as on Earth. Therefore, to make your flight checks on your trip to Mars, you use the same old stars you already know.

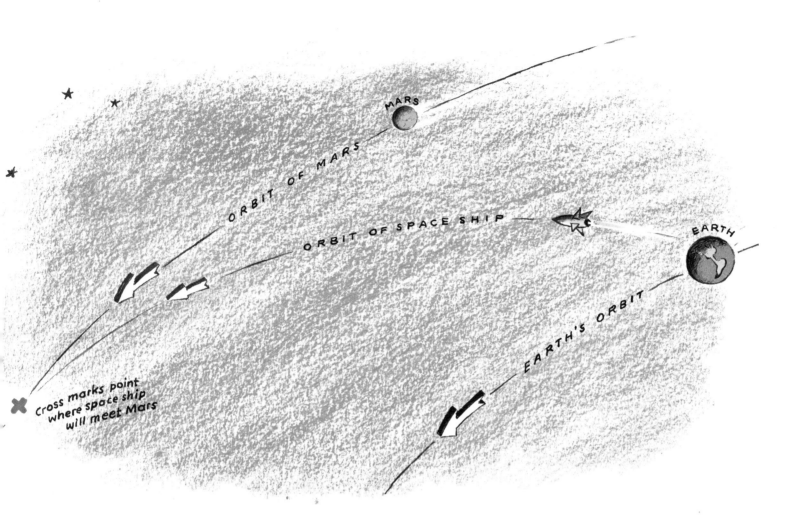

Cross marks point where space ship will meet Mars

If you plan a trip to the moon instead, things would be simpler. The moon is much nearer, of course, so the journey would be much shorter; only a couple of days. But you would still have to intercept the moon. Again you would have to check your flight with the help of the stars and constellations.

It's true—we space skippers must know the constellations! check!

Earth and Stars Seen from the Moon

Earth seen from the moon looks to be more than 13 times as large as the moon seen from Earth. The stars near Earth on this view belong to the Scorpion. Earth seen from the moon is always in or near a constellation of the zodiac, just as the moon seen from the Earth.

To the right and the left are crater-shaped mountains, typical of the moon. Some lunar mountains are very high, up to about 27,000 feet. The moon has no water and very little or no atmosphere, and an observatory there would have to be pressurized and air-conditioned for extreme heat and cold: It's about 215°F in the bright sunshine and about 240°F below zero in the shade.

What's "Lunar"?

Comes from "Luna," Latin for "Moon"!

Mt. Everest is 29,000 feet!

Spaceship Approaching Mars

The spaceship has finished the greater part of its trip and will soon land on Mars. Above Mars are Pollux and Castor, and between Mars and the spaceship are the other stars of the Twins. Procyon, Betelgeuse, and Aldebaran are there too; perhaps you can spot them.

This is a glimpse of what may become a fact in the future. It will be quite a while till man will set foot on Mars, but our astronauts have already visited the moon several times and walked on the lunar surface. Back here on Earth, while many other modern means of navigation now help steer ships and planes, we can always fall back on our faithful guides in the heavens to help us travel by sea, by air, or even in space.

We have finished our trip through the starry skies.

We can now find the constellations, and when we see a bright star at night we shall recognize it and know it by name and greet it as a friend.

This book is only a beginning, of course. It does not tell you all about the stars. No book, even one with hundreds of pages, can tell all that is known about them.

In case you want to know more about stars and planets and galaxies, if you want to find out about eclipses and comets and other things that have to do with the heavens, then get a few more books. Perhaps the ones named below will help you, and there are many others.

On stars and planets:

Solar System
    by Mike Goldsmith. Kingfisher, 2004.

Peterson's First Guide to Astronomy
    by Jay M. Pasachoff. Houghton Mifflin, 1988.

A Field Guide to Stars and Planets, fourth edition
    by Jay M. Pasachoff. Houghton Mifflin, 1999.

On space travel:

Team Moon: How 400,000 People Landed Apollo 11 *on the Moon*
    by Catherine Thimmesh. Houghton Mifflin, 2006.

And now once again, happy stargazing!

Since Venus is so bright that you see her before you see any other star, we won't bother with the constellations she is in. She is either in the west as an evening star or in the east as a morning star, and never very high in the sky. When she changes from evening star to morning star, or vice versa, you won't see her at all for weeks or even months. This is her schedule, for the first of each month (E is for evening star, M is for morning star):

Venus: E: Jan.–Aug. 2007; M: Sept. 2007–May 2008; E: Aug. 2008–Mar. 2009; M: Apr.–Dec. 2009; E: Mar.–Sept. 2010; M: Nov. 2010–July 2011; E: Oct. 2011–May 2012; M: July 2012–Feb. 2013; E: May 2013–Jan. 2014; M: Feb.–Sept. 2014; E: Dec. 2014–Aug. 2015; M: Sept. 2015–May 2016; E: July 2016–Mar. 2017

The constellations in or near which Mars, Jupiter, and Saturn will be from 2007 to 2016 are given for all months of each year, for the first of each month. This does not mean that you can see them at all times. Sometimes they are up in the daytime only, when, of course, they are impossible to see.

2007   **Mars:** Jan., Serpent Holder; Feb., Archer; Mar.–Apr., Goat; May, Water Bearer; June, Fishes; July, Ram; Aug.–Sept., Bull; Oct.–Dec., Twins
       Jupiter: Jan.–Dec., Serpent Holder
       Saturn: Jan.–Dec., Lion

2008   **Mars:** Jan.–Mar., Bull; Apr.–May, Twins; June, Crab; July–Aug., Lion; Sept.–Oct., Virgin; Nov., Scales; Dec., Serpent Holder
       Jupiter: Jan.–Dec., Archer
       Saturn: Jan.–Dec., Lion

2009   **Mars:** Jan.–Feb., Archer; Mar., Goat; Apr., Water Bearer; May, Whale; June–July, Ram; Aug., Bull; Sept.–Oct., Twins; Nov., Crab; Dec., Lion
       Jupiter: Jan., Archer; Feb.–Dec., Goat
       Saturn: Jan.–Sept., Lion; Oct.–Dec., Virgin

2010   **Mars:** Jan., Lion; Feb.–May, Crab; June–July, Lion; Aug.–Sept., Virgin; Oct., Scales; Nov., Scorpion; Dec., Serpent Holder
       Jupiter: Jan., Goat; Feb.–May, Water Bearer; June–Oct., Fishes; Nov.–Dec., Water Bearer
       Saturn: Jan.–Dec., Virgin

2011   **Mars:** Jan., Archer; Feb., Goat; Mar., Water Bearer; Apr.–May, Fishes; June, Ram; July–Aug., Bull; Sept., Twins; Oct., Crab; Nov.–Dec., Lion
       Jupiter: Jan.–Feb., Fishes; Mar., Whale; Apr.–June, Fishes; July–Dec., Ram
       Saturn: Jan –Dec., Virgin

2012   **Mars:** Jan., Lion; Feb., Virgin; Mar.–June, Lion; July–Sept., Virgin; Oct., Scales; Nov., Serpent Holder; Dec., Archer
       Jupiter: Jan., Fishes; Feb.–May, Ram; June–Dec., Bull
       Saturn: Jan.–Dec., Virgin

2013   **Mars:** Jan., Goat; Feb.–Mar., Water Bearer; Apr., Fishes; May, Ram; June–July, Bull; Aug., Twins; Sept., Crab; Oct.–Nov., Lion; Dec., Virgin
       Jupiter: Jan.–June, Bull; July–Dec., Twins
       Saturn: Jan.–May, Scales; June–Aug., Virgin; Sept.–Dec., Scales

2014   **Mars:** Jan.–Aug., Virgin; Sept., Scales; Oct., Serpent Holder; Nov.–Dec., Archer
       Jupiter: Jan.–July, Twins; Aug.–Oct., Crab; Nov.–Dec., Lion
       Saturn: Jan–Dec., Scales

2015   **Mars:** Jan., Goat; Feb., Water Bearer; Mar., Whale; Apr.–May, Ram; June, Bull; July–Aug., Twins; Sept., Crab; Oct., Lion; Nov.–Dec., Virgin
       Jupiter: Jan.–Feb., Lion; Mar.–June, Crab; July–Dec., Lion
       Saturn: Jan., Scales; Feb.–May, Scorpion; June–Oct., Scales; Nov., Scorpion; Dec., Serpent Holder

2016   **Mars:** Jan., Virgin; Feb.–Mar., Scales; Apr.–May, Scorpion; June–Aug., Scales; Sept., Scorpion; Oct.–Nov., Archer; Dec., Goat
       Jupiter: Jan.–Aug., Lion; Sept.–Dec., Virgin
       Saturn: Jan.–Dec., Serpent Holder

And what about the planets after 2016?

Then we'll need a new Planet Finder!

FIRST STARS TO COME OUT AT DUSK

This table is for outdoor use only. Don't bother with it unless you plan to go out at nightfall to look at the sky. It shows the first stars to come out at dusk, about half an hour after sunset throughout the year, on the first of each month, or a few days before and after.

You can see the first bright stars long before it gets dark enough to make out the constellations, and it is fun to identify them as they become visible in the darkening sky. It's special fun to watch a bright star come up above the horizon. This table also tells you where to look for such an event.

The General Sky Chart on page 72 shows you all stars in relation to each other; it will be quite a help. And don't let the planets fool you. This table does not include them. You know why, of course. The Planet Finder tells you where to expect them and when.

January: Capella northeast, rising. Vega northwest, setting. Right of Capella, Aldebaran. Above Vega, Deneb. Left of Vega, Altair. Vega, Altair, Deneb form famous right triangle (the "Summer Triangle," so called) known to all navigators. Watch eastern horizon for Rigel and Betelgeuse, about to rise any minute.

February: Sirius low southeast, rising. Capella high up east. Left of Sirius, Procyon. Above Sirius, Rigel right, Betelgeuse left. Right of Capella, Aldebaran. Below Capella, Pollux and Castor, the Twin stars. In northwest Deneb setting. Note Great Arc of Sirius, formed by Sirius, Procyon, Pollux, Castor, Capella.

March: Sirius southeast. Capella overhead. Rigel and Betelgeuse high to right of Sirius. Procyon left of Sirius. Farther up along Great Arc, Pollux and Castor. High to right above Rigel, Aldebaran. Low east, Regulus rising. Very low northwest, last glimpse of Deneb.

April: Sirius west of south. Capella almost overhead. Right of Sirius, Rigel. Left above Rigel, Betelgeuse. Left above Sirius, Procyon. Farther along Great Arc (see February), Pollux and Castor, almost overhead. Right of Betelgeuse, Aldebaran. High southeast, Regulus. Watch northeast horizon for Arcturus, about to rise.

May: Sirius setting low southwest. Arcturus high east. Capella west, on way down. High left above Sirius, Procyon, and farther along Great Arc (see February), between Procyon and Capella, Pollux and Castor. Right of Sirius, Betelgeuse and farther along Aldebaran. Regulus high up south; Spica southeast to lower right of Arcturus.

June: Arcturus almost overhead. Vega rising northeast. Low northwest, Capella. Low southwest, Procyon. Both setting. Between them, a bit higher, Pollux and Castor.

High southwest, Regulus. Lower right of Arcturus, Spica. Watch horizon for Deneb to rise northeast, left of Vega, and for Antares to rise southeast, far right of Vega.

July: Arcturus almost overhead. Vega high east. Spica to lower right of Arcturus. Regulus west, setting. In south, Antares, distinctly reddish. Lower left of Vega, Deneb. Lower and farther right, Altair. Look for famous "Summer Triangle," a right triangle formed by Vega, Altair, and Deneb.

August: Vega almost overhead. Arcturus high west. Below Vega, Deneb to left, Altair somewhat lower to right. Look for "Summer Triangle" (see July). Reddish Antares south. Spica low southwest, setting.

September: Vega overhead. Arcturus west. Below Vega, Deneb to left, Altair somewhat lower to right. Look for "Summer Triangle" (see above). Reddish Antares low south. Farther right Spica, setting southwest.

October: Vega overhead. Arcturus west, setting. Below Vega, Deneb high in east, Altair high in south. Look for "Summer Triangle" (which remains visible till Jan.). Reddish Antares low southwest, setting. Low southeast, Fomalhaut rising, announcing that fall has come.

November: Vega almost overhead. Arcturus low northwest, about to dip below horizon. Deneb overhead, Altair high southwest. Look for "Summer Triangle" (see above). Fomalhaut low in southeast. Watch northeast horizon for Capella, about to rise.

December: Vega high west. Capella low northeast, going up. Above Vega, Deneb, almost overhead. Lower left of Vega, Altair. Look for "Summer Triangle," the right triangle formed by Vega, Altair, and Deneb. Watch horizon in east for Aldebaran, about to rise.

Can I use these tables any year?

66

TIME TABLE FOR SKY VIEWS

This table shows you which sky view to use and at which hour to use it, for any night of the year. All hours are your own Standard Time. If you are on Daylight Saving Time, add one hour: for 7 p.m. read 8 p.m., and so on.

around		use Sky View	about		around		use Sky View	about
Jan.	1	4,	6 p.m.		July	1	3,	11 p.m.
	or	1,	11 p.m.		July	15	3,	10 p.m.
Jan.	15	4,	5 p.m.		Aug.	1	3,	9 p.m.
	or	1,	10 p.m.		Aug.	15	3,	8 p.m.
Feb.	1	1,	9 p.m.		Sept.	1	3,	7 p.m.
Feb.	15	1,	8 p.m.			or	4,	1 a.m.
Mar.	1	1,	7 p.m.		Sept.	15	4,	midnight
Mar.	15	1,	6 p.m.		Oct.	1	4,	11 p.m.
	or	2,	midnight		Oct.	15	4,	10 p.m.
Apr.	1	2,	11 p.m.		Nov.	1	4,	9 p.m.
Apr.	15	2,	10 p.m.		Nov.	15	4,	8 p.m.
May	1	2,	9 p.m.		Dec.	1	4,	7 p.m.
May	15	2,	8 p.m.		Dec.	15	4,	6 p.m.
June	1	3,	1 a.m.			or	1,	midnight
June	15	3,	midnight					

THE 15 BRIGHTEST STARS

visible in all of the U.S.; in order of brightness.

Sirius in Big Dog, bluish, distance 8½ light-years
Arcturus in Herdsman, orange, 32 light-years
Vega in Lyre, bluish white, 23 light-years
Capella in Charioteer, yellowish, 42 light-years
Rigel in Orion, bluish white, 545 light-years
Procyon in Little Dog, yellowish white, 10 light-years
Betelgeuse in Orion, reddish, 300 light-years
Altair in Eagle, yellowish white, 18 light-years
Aldebaran in Bull, reddish, 54 light-years
Antares in Scorpion, reddish, 170 light-years
Spica in Virgin, bluish, 190 light-years
Pollux in Twins, yellowish, 31 light-years
Fomalhaut in Southern Fish, white, 27 light-years
Deneb in Swan, white, 465 light-years
Regulus in Lion, bluish white, 70 light-years

Visible only in the southern U.S.:

Canopus in Ship's Keel, yellowish white, 650 light-years, brighter than Vega, second only to Sirius.

You can use them a hundred years if you live that long!

INDEX AND GLOSSARY

but we now know they are not; 64

Constellation, group of stars forming a certain shape and having a name of its own; 7, 10, 24–25. There are 88 constellations in the entire sky but about 30 cannot be seen in our mid-northern latitudes (about 40° north).

Corona Australis, Latin for Southern Crown

Corona Borealis (stress on *al*), Latin for Northern Crown

Corvus, Latin for Crow

Crab (Latin: Cancer), constellation in zodiac; 28–29, 35, 38–39

Crane (Latin: Grus), southern constellation, only partly visible in most of U.S.; 53

Crater, Latin for Cup

Crow (Latin: Corvus), constellation near Virgin; 38–39

Crux, Latin for Southern Cross

Cup (Latin: Crater), small constellation on the back of Hydra, the Water Snake; 38–39

Cygnus, Latin for Swan

Delphinus (stress on *phi*), Latin for Dolphin

Deneb (Arabic for tail), 1st-mag. star in Swan, white, 465 light-years away; 20, 23, 33, 36–37, 44–45, 50–51, 66, 67

Doctor in the Sky, see Serpent Holder

Dolphin (Latin: Delphinus), small constellation near Eagle's head; 46–47, 52–53

Dove (Latin: Columba), small constellation south of Orion; 28–29

Dragon (Latin: Draco), constellation near Pole Star; 26–27, 32, 33, 36–37, 44–45, 50–51

Eagle (Latin: Aquila, stress on *Aq*), summer constellation with 1st-mag. star Altair; 20, 22, 23, 46–47, 52–53

Earth, planet, 3rd from the sun; 56–58, 60, 61, 62

Ecliptic (dotted line on General Sky Chart, p. 72), sun's path among the constellations. If we could see the stars in daytime, we should see the sun slowly wander from one constellation of the zodiac to the next, making one complete round in one year. Ecliptic runs along middle of zodiac. When the moon gets into Ecliptic (it often does), exactly between Earth and the sun, it hides the sun for a short while, and we get an eclipse of the sun. Hence the name Ecliptic (place where eclipses occur). When Earth gets exactly between the sun and moon, we have an eclipse of the moon.

Eridanus (stress on *rid*), Latin name for The River

Evening Star, see Stars

Fishes (Latin: Pisces, stress on *Pis*), constellation in zodiac; 26–27, 28–29, 35, 44–45, 52–53

Fomalhaut (Arabic: Fish's Mouth, stress on *Fom*), 1st-mag. star in Southern Fish; white, 27 light-years away; 21, 52–53, 66, 67

Galaxy, Greek for Milky Way; also, enormous swarms of billions of stars floating in space. Our solar system and all stars we see in the sky belong to such a galaxy, and there are billions of other galaxies; 50–53. See also Milky Way

Gemini (stress on *Gem*), Latin for Twins

Gemma (Latin for Gem), 2nd-mag. star in Northern Crown; 36–37, 38–39, 46–47

Giraffe (Latin: Camelopardalis, stress on *pard*), faint constellation near Pole Star; 26–27, 32, 33, 36–37, 44–45, 50–51

Goat (Latin: Capricornus, stress on *corn*), constellation in zodiac; 35, 46–47, 52–53

Great Arc of Sirius, see Sirius

Great Bear (Latin: Ursa Major), large constellation of which Big Dipper is part; 7, 26–27, 33, 36–37, 38–39, 44–45, 50–51

Great Square of Pegasus, large square formed by four stars of Pegasus and Andromeda; landmark of autumn sky; 26–27, 41, 44–45, 52–53. See also Pegasus

Greek, the ancient Greeks were great astronomers. We still use many names the Greeks gave to stars and constellations. The word "astronomy" is Greek too.

Hare (Latin: Lepus), small constellation below Orion's feet; 28–29, 42, 43

Hercules (stress on *Her*), large but faint constellation near Dragon's head, named after Greek hero; 36–37, 44–45, 46–47, 50–51

Herdsman (Greek: Böötes, stress on second *o*), constellation with 1st-mag. star Arcturus; 8, 11, 18, 19, 26–27, 33, 36–37, 38–39, 44–45, 46–47, 50–51

Horse and Rider star, middle star in Big Dipper's handle (2nd-mag., Mizar by name), has faint star very close by (named Alcor). The two are often called "Horse and Rider." The ancients used them as eye test—if you could see both your vision was all right; 6, 7, 26–27, 36–37, 44–45, 50–51

Hunting Dogs (Latin: Canes Venatici, stress on *nat*), small constellation near Great Bear; 26–27, 36–37, 38–39, 44–45

Hydra, the Water Snake; long, faint constellation below Virgin, with 2nd-mag. star Alphard; 28–29, 38–39

Juno, ancient goddess, Jupiter's wife; 42. One of the larger asteroids is named after her

Jupiter, chief of ancient gods; 42. Largest planet is named after him; 55–59, 65

Lacerta, Latin for Lizard

Latitude, distance of a place from Earth's equator, to the north or south, in degrees. It depends on your latitude what stars you can see, therefore latitude is important for stargazers. On latitude 40° north (latitude of Philadelphia) about one-ninth of the entire sky remains always below the horizon and cannot be seen. The charts in this book are designed for 40° latitude north, because the greater part of our population lives near that latitude; 29, 33

Leo, Latin for Lion

Leo Minor, Latin for Little Lion

Lepus, Latin for Hare

Libra, Latin for Scales

Light-year, the distance light travels in a year. Light travels 186,000 miles a second, or almost six million million miles a year; light-years are used to measure distances of stars; 14, 15

faint constellation above Scorpion, "Doctor in the Sky"; 38–39, 42, 43, 46–47, 52–53

Ship (Argo, ship of the Greek hero Jason), large constellation in southern sky; not wholly visible in our latitudes; has four parts: Sail, Stern, Keel, and Compass; in Ship's Keel is 1st-mag. star Canopus (stress on *no*), 2nd-brightest star in the sky, yellowish white, 650 light-years away, visible only in the southern U.S.; 28–29, 38–39

Shooting Stars, also called Meteors; not stars at all, but small lumps of matter falling to Earth from outer space at enormous speed; set aglow by friction with Earth's atmosphere—that's why we see them as sparks shooting across the sky. Most disintegrate under way, but some reach the ground: those are called meteorites; 55

Sirius, 1st-mag. star in Big Dog, brightest star in the sky; bluish; 8½ light-years away; 15, 16, 17, 19, 21, 28–29, 66, 67. *Great Arc of Sirius* is huge arc in the sky, formed by five stars: Sirius, Procyon, Pollux, Castor, Capella; easy to find, helps spot constellations near it; 28–29, 67

Solar System (solar from sol, Latin for Sun), the sun and its planets with their satellites, asteroids, and comets—all revolving around it; 57

Southern Cross (Latin: Crux), famous southern constellation, not visible in our latitudes; 31

Southern Crown (Latin: Corona Australis), faint constellation near Archer; 46–47

Southern Fish (Latin: Piscis Austrinus, stress on *tri*), small constellation, with 1st-mag. star Fomalhaut; 21, 52–53

Space Probe Mariner 4 took first close-up pictures of planet Mars (July 1965); 59

Spica, 1st-mag. star in Virgin, bluish, 190 light-years away; 17, 23, 38–39, 46–47, 66, 67

Stars, heavenly bodies; all stars that we see with the naked eye are globes of fiery gas tremendously large and hot, most of them larger than our sun, which is also a star. Many stars are smaller than the sun (some even smaller than the planet Jupiter) and some are cold and dark, but we can't see these without telescopes. There are over a hundred billion stars in our galaxy alone, but with the naked eye we only see about 2,500 at any time, under best conditions.
15 brightest stars; 21, 67. *First stars to come out*; 39, 66
Fixed Stars, or *True Stars*, all stars are true stars except the planets, which are not really stars; 56
Star Colors; 17, 45. Star colors are faint, but with a little practice you distinguish them well.
Morning Star, Evening Star; not a true star but a planet when it shines brightly, low above the horizon, at daybreak or at nightfall; most often it is Venus, but Mars, Jupiter, and Saturn can also be morning or evening stars; 55
Star Names, 11; most star names are Arabic, Greek, or Latin.
Star Schedule, 48–49

"Summer Triangle," a right triangle formed by three 1st-mag. stars—Vega, Altair, and Deneb—known to all navigators. In our latitudes you see it July-Jan.; 46, 47, 66

Sun, a star, center of our solar system; 15, 56–59

Swan (Latin: Cygnus), constellation with 1st-mag. star Deneb; 20, 22, 23, 33, 36–37, 44–45, 46–47, 50–51; its five brightest stars form a large cross, known as the Northern Cross.

Taurus, Latin for Bull

Triangle (Latin: Triangulum, stress on *ang*), small constellation near Milky Way; 26–27, 50–51, 52–53

Triangle of Vega, see Vega

Twins (Latin: Gemini, stress on *Gem*), constellation in zodiac, with 1st-mag. star Pollux and 2nd-mag. star Castor; 12, 18, 19, 28–29, 36–37, 38–39, 50–51, 63

Unicorn (Greek: Monoceros, stress on *no*), faint constellation near Orion

Uranus (stress on *U*), planet, seventh from the sun; 56, 57, 59

Ursa Major, Latin for Great Bear

Ursa Minor, Latin for Little Bear (Little Dipper)

Vega, 1st-mag. star in Lyre, bluish white, 23 light-years away; 20, 21, 23, 33, 36–37, 44–45, 46–47, 50–51, 66, 67; Vega was first star to have its photograph taken, in 1850. *Triangle of Vega*, right triangle formed by three 1st-.mag. stars: Vega, Deneb, Altair; right angle is at Vega; Vega's triangle is famous, used by all navigators; not to be mixed up with constellation called Triangle, which is small and unimportant; 46–47, 72

Venus, neighbor planet of Earth, 2nd from the sun; 55–58, 65

Virgin (Latin: Virgo), constellation in zodiac, with 1st-mag. star Spica, bluish, 190 light-years away; 17, 22, 23, 38–39, 46–47

Water Carrier (Latin: Aquarius, stress on *qua*), constellation in zodiac; 35, 46–47, 52–53

Whale (Latin: Cetus), large constellation but faint; 29, 40, 41, 52–53

Wolf (Latin: Lupus), southern constellation, only his rear end visible in most of U.S.; 46–47

Year, time it takes a planet to go around the sun once; 57–59

Zenith, point in the sky directly overhead; 45

Zodiac (stress on *Zo*; Greek, meaning Animal Circle), belt around the sky formed by 12 constellations, important because the planets are always seen in or near a zodiac constellation, and the same goes for the moon, as you can check for yourself; 12, 17, 20, 34–35, 55, 56, 60–61
The 12 constellations, in the order in which they are in the sky: Ram, Bull, Twins, Crab, Lion, Virgin, Scales, Scorpion, Archer, Goat, Water Carrier, Fishes.
Jingle to memorize the 12 zodiac constellations:
The ramble twins crab liverish,
Scaly scorpions are good waterfish.
(Ram; ble for Bull; Twins; Crab; li for Lion; ver for Virgin; scaly for Scales; Scorpion; are for Archer; good for Goat; water for Water Carrier: fish for Fishes)

71

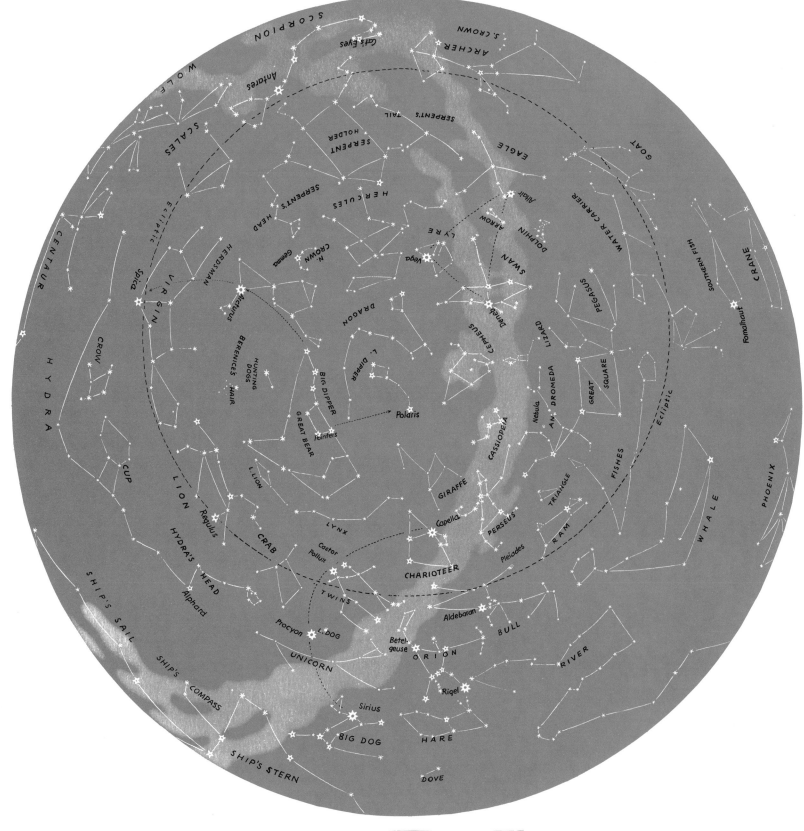

GENERAL SKY CHART

This chart shows all constellations that can be seen in most of the U.S. Not all
constellations can be seen at the same time. It depends on the hour of night and
time of year which constellations are up and can be seen, and which are below the
horizon and cannot be seen. The sky views show which are up at what time.